CAKES & SWEETS GRAPHICS
VISUAL PROMOTION FOR THE CONFECTIONERY INDUSTRY

CAKES & SWEETS GRAPHICS
VISUAL PROMOTION FOR THE CONFECTIONERY INDUSTRY

ISBN 4-938812-29-0 C3070 P16000E
First edition, September 1995
Printed in Japan
MEISEI PUBLICATIONS
#203, 3-11-1 Kanda, Jinbo-cho, Chiyoda-ku, Tokyo 101, Japan
Phone (03)5276-1941 Facsimile (03)5276-1966

CAKES & SWEETS GRAPHICS
VISUAL PROMOTION FOR THE CONFECTIONERY INDUSTRY

MEISEI
Publications

CONTENTS

スィート ショップ グラフィックス

CAKES & SWEETS GRAPHICS

PREFACE

　日本の洋菓子は、戦国末期にオランダ人やポルトガル人などによって伝来されて以後、日本人の生活に密接に関わってきました。金平糖やマルボウロ、カステラなどですが、これらは伝来当初より日本人の味覚に合わせ、日本風に改良されて、長くわれわれの楽しみとなってきました。一方、明治維新による文明開化は、それらの洋菓子とは別の、新しい菓子の風土を日本にもたらしました。ビスケットやアイスクリーム、シュークリームやチョコレート、マシュマロやキャンディーなどがそれです。これらもいまやお菓子の代表として世代を問わず、われわれの生活になじみ深いものとなっています。

　戦国期より数えて500年、明治維新からは130年の歴史を有する日本の洋菓子ですが、近年は、食文化の多様化とともに味はもちろん消費者自身の嗜好も変わり、菓子メーカーは従来の伝統を受け継ぐとともに、菓子の種類やかたち、味など、じつにさまざまな工夫をこらしています。また、経済大国となった日本では、消費者がその豊かさの中で違和感もなく欧米の食文化を味わい、菓子を口にし、本物の味を知るようになってきました。メーカーサイドもその要求に応え、いまや日本は世界でも有数の菓子文化を謳歌しています。最近では、欧米のメーカーも日本に進出するようになってきました。これらの洋菓子に負けず劣らず、和菓子も百花繚乱、培われた伝統のうえに新しさを加え、日本の菓子文化の大きな流れを形作っています。

　本書では、これらの豊かに花開いた日本の菓子文化の中で、洋菓子を中心に和菓子も含め、そのグラフィックとしての表現であるカタログ・パンフレット・パッケージなどのデザインを紹介します。販促用としてのカタログ・パンフレットをはじめ、お菓子の味やかたちを包むパッケージ・包装紙などは、細やかに、そして確実に、店々によって受け継がれてきたお菓子のイメージを伝えています。カタログのかたちの面白さ、使う用紙のふうあいをはじめ、写真やイラスト、さらには配色と、さまざまなデザインが工夫され、それだけでも密度の濃い、ハイレベルなものとなっています。これらのグラフィック作品は、その実用性はもちろんのこと、さらに一歩進んで、広くお菓子の味わいにまでも直接、影響を及ぼしていることはたしかでしょう。

　本書では、これらのグラフィック作品をとおして、日本の菓子文化の現在と、そのデザイン表現の最前線を紹介できると考えております。1冊の書籍としてはわが国ではじめての試みであり、読者の方々のご批評を俟ちたいと思います。

　最後に、本書を刊行するにあたって、快くグラフィック作品等をご提供いただいた菓子製造・販売各社のみなさま、デザイン制作者の方々に、厚くお礼を申し上げます。

スィート ショップ グラフィックス
編集プロジェクト

Confectionery has played an important part in the daily life of the Japanese people since confeito,bolo,castella and so forth were first introduced into Japan by the Dutch and Portuguese during the late 16th century. After their tastes were adjusted to match our preferences,they have been loved by the Japanese people ever since then. Later, after the Meiji Restoration(1868), different varieties of sweets were again introduced from overseas and became widespread among the people through the effects of civilization and enlightenment. Biscuits, ice cream, cream parfait, chocolates,marshmallow and other candies have become a familiar part of the daily lives of people of all generations.

The Japanese manufacturers of confectionery, which have their own history of 500 years since the late 16th century and for 130 years since the Meiji Restoration, have maintained their own traditions while contributing to the production of a diversity of new tastes and shapes in confectionery products in order to be able to cope with the diversifying food culture and changes in consumer tastes. As Japan has developed into a major economic power in the world today, we are fortunate to have many chances and places to savor real Western foods including confectionery. The confectionery manufacturers have been working hard to offer high-quality products to the consumers and have now established the highest level of confectionery culture in Japan. European and American confectionery manufacturers have also expanded their business to cover Japan in order to capture the Japanese consumers. Today, the Japanese traditional sweets as well as the Western-style confectionery are flourishing in Japan. The manufacturers are creating new styles on top of the existing traditions and are playing an important role in leading the Japanese confectionery cuiture. The current prosperity of the Japanese confectionery culture has been established by these two types of sweets.

This book of the confectionery catalog graphics presents a collection of excellent graphic design items such as the brochures, pamphlets and wrappers used in the sales promotion of both the Western and Japanese confectionery. These graphic items express the delicate image of products that each manufacturer has inherited from its founder. The shapes and materials of paper,photographs and illustrations, colors of these items, we believe, demonstrate an advanced sense of design. Such items have been proven to be highly successful in advertising. Furthermore, they are also greatly instrumental in helping people enjoy the taste of confectionery.

In this book, we introduce the current status of the confectionery culture in Japan and the most up-to-date design sensitivity through confectionery-related graphic works. Since this is the first issue of confectionery catalog graphics, we would highly appreciate any comments that you, the readers, may have.

Finally, we would like to express our gratitude to the confectionery manufacturers and their sales and design departments, whose cooperation and offers of materials have been indispansable in the publication of this book.

The Editors
CAKES & SWEETS GRAPHICS

Abbreviations

PL Planner   LD Logotype designer D Designer   PH Photographer
AD Art director   IL Illustrator   CW Copywriter   PD Producer

WESTERN CONFECTIONERIES

洋菓子

CAKES

フランセ
FRANÇAIS

PL 綿屋喜兵衛(株)
AD 綿屋喜兵衛(株)
D 綿屋喜兵衛(株)

PL WATAKI Co., Ltd.
AD WATAKI Co., Ltd.
D WATAKI Co., Ltd.

1

1. パンフレット

1. Brochures

2. 菓子箱、パンフレット

2. Box, brochures

3

3. ショップバッグ、菓子箱、パンフレット

3. Shopping bag, boxes, brochures

4

5

6. 菓子箱、リボン、パンフレット

6. Box, streamer, brochures

7

8

7. 菓子箱、栞
8. ケーキ缶、包装紙

7. Box, product guide
8. A can for cakes, wrapping paper

CAKES

アンリ・シャルパンティエ
HENRI CHARPENTIER

PL （株）アンリ・シャルパンティエ
CW （株）二人のデスク、蟻田善造
AD イナ商會、稲田　明
D イナ商會、稲田　明

PL HENRI CHARPENTIER Co., Ltd.
CW Zenzo Arita, Futari no Desk Co., Ltd.
AD Akira Inada, Ina Shokai
D Akira Inada, Ina Shokai

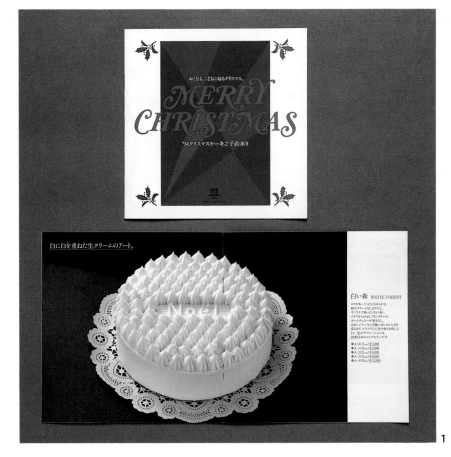

1

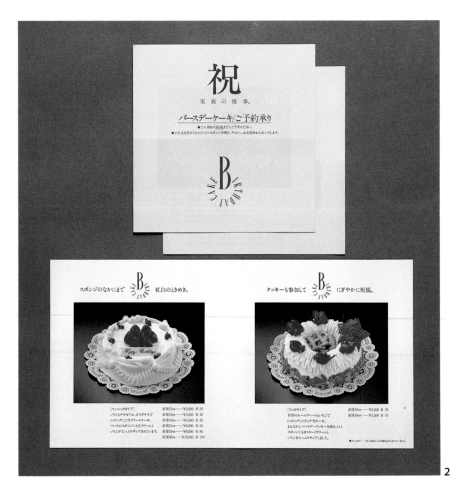

1,2. パンフレット

1,2. Brochures

2

芦屋の
ケーキ、ケーキ、ケーキ

芦屋のフィナンシェ＆マドレーヌ3箱詰合せ SIDE BY SIDE

芦屋市公光町7-10-101　　アンリ・シャルパンティエ

フィナンシェ＆マドレーヌ詰合せ TWO IN ONE

3, 4. 菓子箱
3, 4. Boxes

17

5. 菓子箱
PL （株）アンリ・シャルパンティエ
CW （株）二人のデスク、蟻田善造
AD 川畑直道
D 川畑直道

5. Boxes
PL HENRI CHARPENTIER Co., Ltd.
CW Zenzo Arita, Futari no Desk Co., Ltd.
AD Naomichi Kawahata
D Naomichi Kawahata

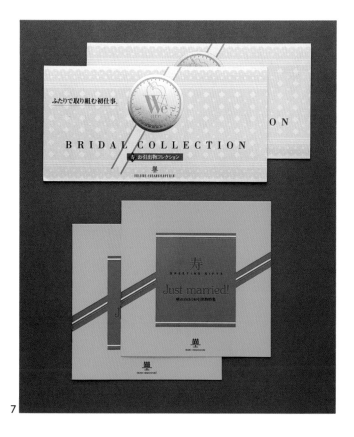

7

地球をいたわるギフト。Salon de Terre

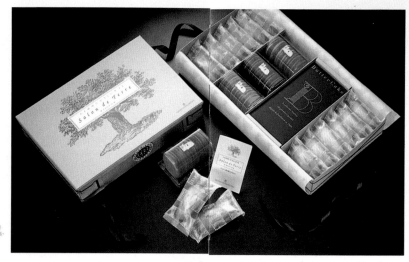

[サロン・ド・テール]
猫マークで愛されたC.C.クッキーと、芦屋のケーキを
ボリュームたっぷり詰め合わせ。
いずれも自然素材にこだわった焼き菓子で、
いわばこの大地が生みの親です。
そのため地球へのいたわりをこめ、パッケージに
エコ素材を使用して省資源のお手つだいをします。
●Sボックス──────¥3,000　ST-30
（フィナンシェ、マドレーヌ各5コ/C.C.クッキー18枚）
●Lボックス──────¥5,000　ST-50
（バターケーキ1本/フィナンシェ、
マドレーヌ各6コ/C.C.クッキー18枚）

エコマインドを大切に。クリーンに焼却できるエコ素材と再生紙を使用したギフトセットです。

6, 7. パンフレット

6, 7. Brochures

8

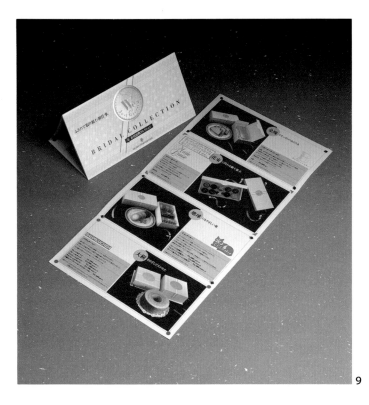

9

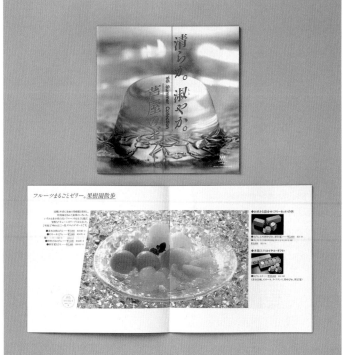

10

8, 10. パンフレット

8, 10. Brochures

9. パンフレット
PL （株）アンリ・シャルパンティエ
CW （株）二人のデスク、蟻田善造
AD 川畑直道
D 川畑直道

9. Brochures
PL HENRI CHARPENTIER Co., Ltd.
CW Zenzo Arita, Futari no Desk Co., Ltd.
AD Naomichi Kawahata
D Naomichi Kawahata

11. 菓子箱

11. Boxes

CAKES

マキシム・ド・パリ
MAXIM'S DE PARIS

1

PL　マキシム・ド・パリ（株）

AD　マキシム・ド・パリ（株）

D　マキシム・ド・パリ（株）、芳本武始

PL　MAXIM'S DE PARIS Ltd.

AD　MAXIM'S DE PARIS Ltd.

D　Takeshi Yoshimoto, MAXIM'S DE
　　PARIS Ltd.

1.　パッケージ、チラシ、バレンタインカード

1.　Packages, flyer, information cards

生 菓 子

❀❀❀ マキシムに咲く名花 ❀❀❀

「デザートを持ち帰りたい……。」

マキシム・ド・パリでお食事を楽しまれたお客様から、
こんな要望がよくあります。
それにお応えしたのが、
ここにご紹介するパティスリーです。
"お菓子の芸術家"が、厳選した材料を用いて
すべて手づくりで仕上げました。
レストラン「マキシム・ド・パリ」の心が、味が、
そのまま生きています。

MAXIM'S
DE PARIS

成させました。2本、3本の
詰合の小箱との組み合わせまで幅広くご用意
致しております。

MAXIM'S
DE PARIS

販売期間5月頃−9月頃

MAXIM'S
DE PARIS

す。なお、小
ます。（1箱¥970）
❀フルーツケーキとの詰め合わせも出来ます。オ...
はフルーツケーキのリーフをご覧下さい。

MAXIM'S
DE PARIS

・ロングラッセ

❀❀❀ 原点

マロングラッセ
厳選されたフラ
バニラ風味のコ...
ズ、あくまで蓄
逸品です。

クッキー
アーモン
ラ、ジン...
と思われ
シムの
菓子の

2. 菓子箱、栞

2. Box, sheets

CAKES

3

4

3. 菓子箱
4. パンフレット
3. Boxes
4. Brochures

24

今田美奈子
ティーサロン
（原宿・薔薇の館）
**MINAKO IMADA
TEA SALON
(HARAJUKU-BARA
NO YAKATA)**

1. パンフレット
PL （有）今田美奈子お菓子教室
AD （株）ポイントライン
D　（株）ポイントライン

1. Brochures
PL　Minako Imada Cake School Ltd.
AD　Point & Line Co., Ltd.
D　　Point & Line Co., Ltd.

2. パンフレット
PL （有）今田美奈子お菓子教室
AD （有）スタジオ・クラスター
D 　（有）スタジオ・クラスター

2. Brochures
PL Minako Imada Cake School Ltd.
AD Studio CLUSTER Ltd.
D 　Studio CLUSTER Ltd.

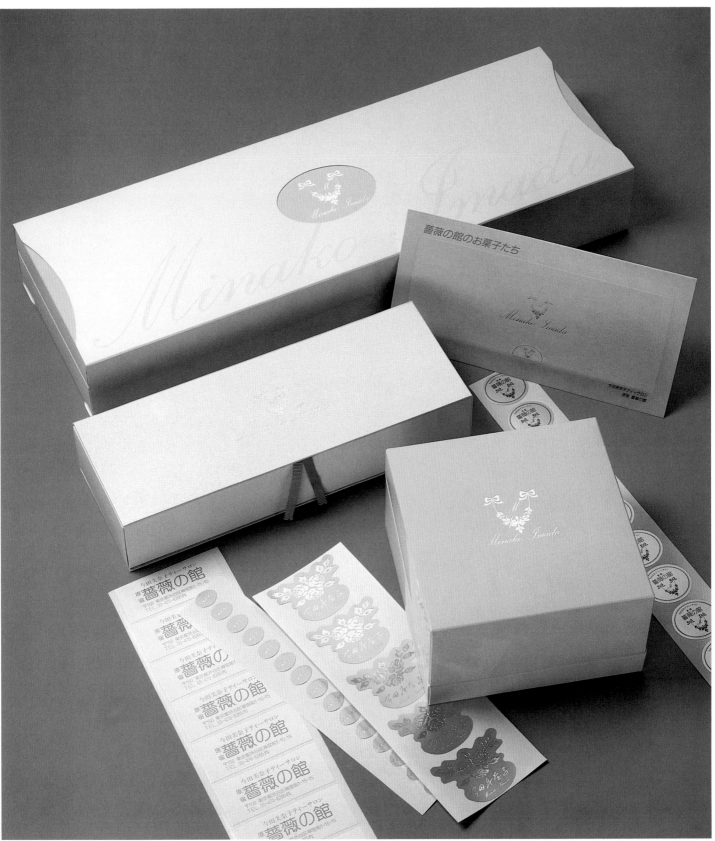

3

菓子箱（上）
PL （有）今田美奈子お菓子教室
AD （株）こふれ
D （株）こふれ

Box (top)
PL Minako Imada Cake School Ltd.
AD Coffret Co., Ltd.
D Coffret Co., Ltd.

菓子箱（中、下）
PL （有）今田美奈子お菓子教室
AD （株）ラグタイム
D （株）ラグタイム

Boxes (middle, bottom)
PL Minako Imada Cake School Ltd.
AD RAGTIME Co., Ltd.
D RAGTIME Co., Ltd.

パンフレット
PL （有）今田美奈子お菓子教室
AD （有）スタジオ・クラスター
D （有）スタジオ・クラスター

Brochure
PL Minako Imada Cake School Ltd.
AD Studio CLUSTER Ltd.
D Studio CLUSTER Ltd.

シール
PL （株）ラグタイム
AD （株）ラグタイム
D （株）ラグタイム

Seals
PL RAGTIME Co., Ltd.
AD RAGTIME Co., Ltd.
D RAGTIME Co., Ltd.

CAKES

シベール
SIBELLE

PL （株）二幸
AD （株）二幸

PL NIKO Co., Ltd.
AD NIKO Co., Ltd.

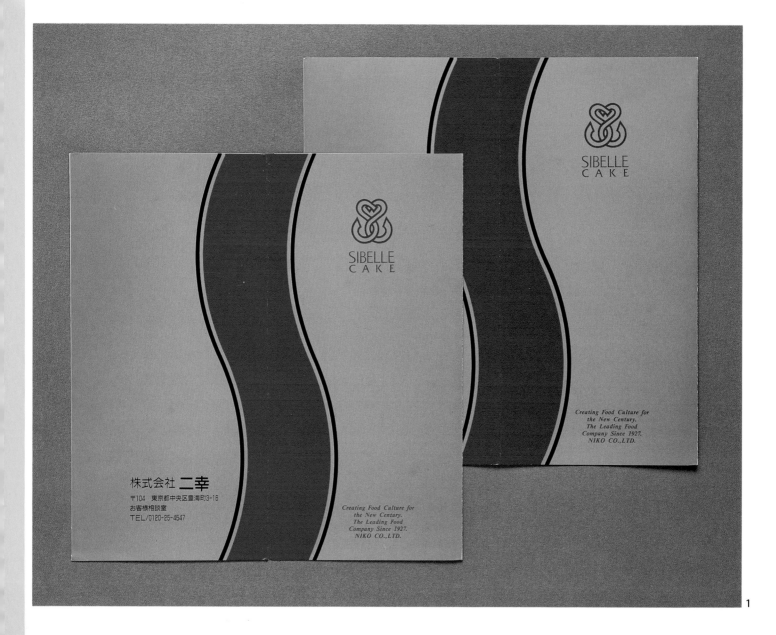

1

1. パンフレット

1. Brochures

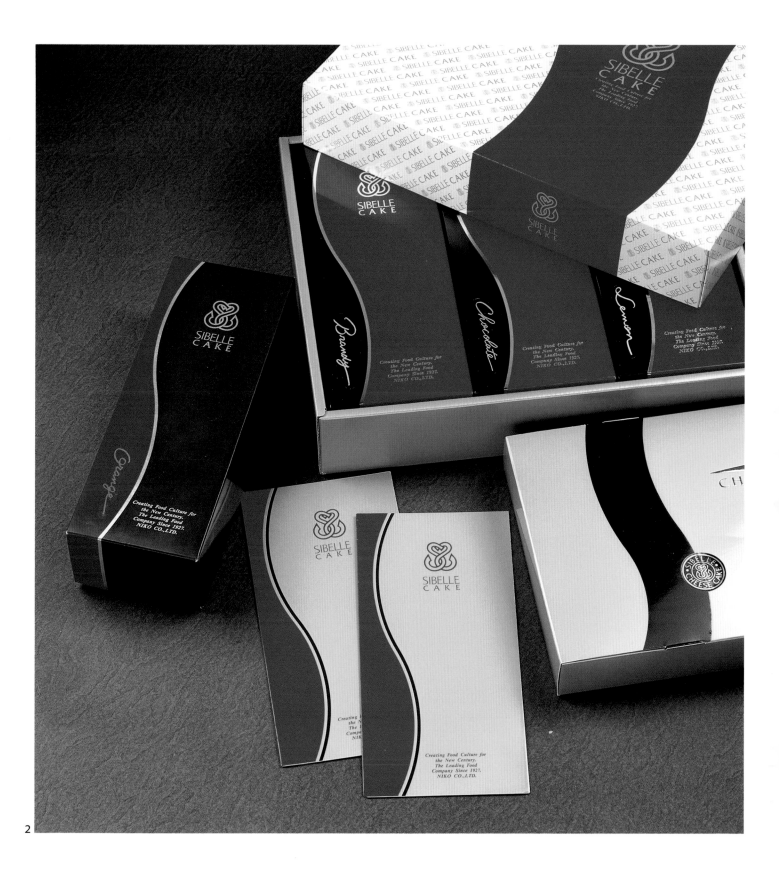

2. パンフレット、菓子箱

2. Brochures, boxes

3. 菓子箱、パンフレット

3. Box, brochures

エーデルワイス
EDELWEISS

PL　(株)スイス菓子エーデルワイス企画部
AD　(株)スイス菓子エーデルワイス企画部
D　(株)スイス菓子エーデルワイス企画部

PL　Planning Division, Edelweiss Co., Ltd.
AD　Planning Division, Edelweiss Co., Ltd.
D　Planning Division, Edelweiss Co., Ltd.

1,2. パンフレット
1,2. Brochures

アンテノール
ANTENOR

PL　（株）アンテノール企画部
AD　（株）アンテノール企画部
D　（株）アンテノール企画部

PL　Planning Division, Antenor Co., Ltd.
AD　Planning Division, Antenor Co., Ltd.
D　Planning Division, Antenor Co., Ltd.

1,2.　パンフレット
1,2.　Brochures

3. 菓子箱、シール

3. Boxes, seals

フレイバー
FLAVOR

PL　（株）フレイバーユージ、岩田有司
AD　（株）フレイバーユージ、岩田有司
D　　（株）フレイバーユージ、岩田有司

PL　Yuji Iwata, FLAVOR　Yuji Co., Ltd.
AD　Yuji Iwata, FLAVOR　Yuji Co., Ltd.
D　　Yuji Iwata, FLAVOR　Yuji Co., Ltd.

1

1. パンフレット

1. Brochures

2. パンフレット、ショップカード
2. Brochures, business cards

CAKES

ドゥバイヨル
DEBAILLEUL

パンフレット
AD 片岡物産（株）、栗本建
D （有）エンゲルス事務所、石田正皇

Brochures
AD Ken Kurimoto, KATAOKA & Co.,Ltd.
D Masatoshi Isida,Creative
　Office Engels Ltd.

菓子箱
D マルク & ネリー・ドゥバイヨル

Boxes
D Marc & Nelly DEBAILLEUL

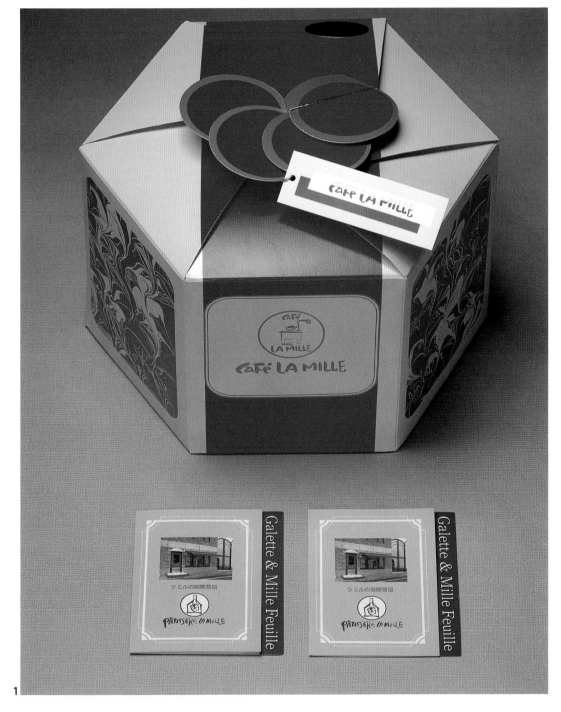

カフェ ラ ミル
CAFÉ LA MILLE

PL　ゼフィルス（株）
AD　ゼフィルス（株）
D　　近藤なおみ

PL　ZEPHILS Co., Ltd.
AD　ZEPHILS Co., Ltd.
D　　Naomi Kondo

1. 菓子箱、パンフレット

1. Box, brochures

CAKES

パティスリー キハチ
PATISSRIE KIHACHI

PL （株）キハチ アンド エス
AD （株）キハチ アンド エス
D （株）キハチ アンド エス

PL KIHACHI & S Co., Ltd.
AD KIHACHI & S Co., Ltd.
D   KIHACHI & S Co., Ltd.

1

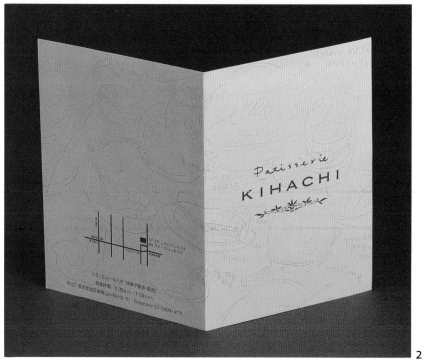

2

1. 商品カタログ
2. パンフレット

1. Product catalog
2. Brochures

シェ松尾
CHEZ MATSUO

PL （株）松尾企画
AD 石川恵津子
D 畠山博子

PL Matsuo Planning Co., Ltd.
AD Etsuko Ishikawa
D Hiroko Hatakeyama

1. パンフレット、カップ

1. Brochures, cup and saucer

2. ショップバッグ

2. Shopping bags

3. 菓子箱、包装紙、テイクアウト用菓子箱
4. パンフレット
3. Boxes, wrapping paper, take-out bag for cakes
4. Brochures

CHEZ MATSUO

1980

CHEZ MATSUO
LA SAVEUR IDEALE ET LA
BEAUTE SUPREME

5. 菓子箱、ショップカード
5. Box, business cards

6. パッケージ、シール、リボン
6. Packages, seals, ribbon

5

6

ポニー
PONY

PL （株）ミックビジネスシステム、内海悟
AD （株）水野肇デザインハウス、水野肇
D 山本徹

PL Satoru Utsumi, MIC Business
Systems Co., Ltd.
AD Hajime Mizuno, Mizuno Design
House Co., Ltd.
D Tohru Yamamoto

1. クッキー缶、パンフレット
1. A can for cookies, brochures

Fruit
SWEET NIGHT

Chocolate
SWEET NIGHT

Cherry
SWEET NIGHT

4. 菓子箱、シール、ショップカード

4. Box, seals, business cards

5. 菓子箱、缶

5. Boxes, a can for cookies

ポンム アリス
POMME ALICE

PL 中瀬薫
D 中瀬薫

PL Kaoru Nakase
D Kaoru Nakase

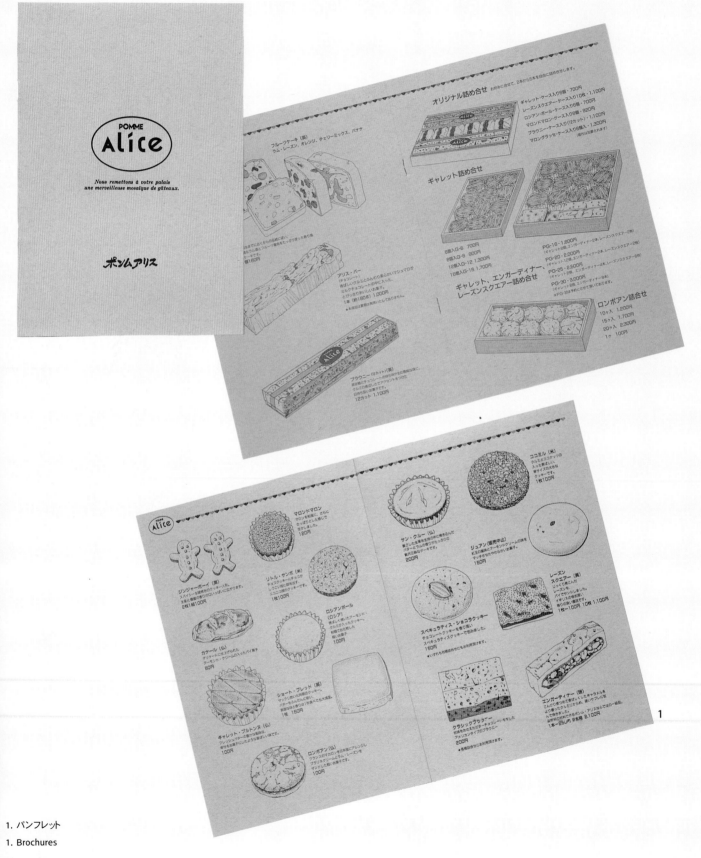

1. パンフレット

1. Brochures

2

2. 菓子箱、包装紙

2. Boxes, wrapping paper

COOKIES

一番館
ICHIBANKAN

PL （株）一番館
AD （株）一番館

PL ICHIBANKAN Co., Ltd.
AD ICHIBANKAN Co., Ltd.

1. パンフレット、菓子袋

1. Brochures, paper bag for cookies

1

2

COOKIES

池ノ上ピエール
IKENOUE PIERRE

PL 鈴木敏郎
PH 小川静雄
D 鈴木敏郎

PL Toshiro Suzuki
PH Shizuo Ogawa
D Toshiro Suzuki

1,2. パンフレット

1,2. Brochures

1

Pâtisserie de l'Alsace de Obernai â Tokyo
アルザスの菓子 オベルネから東京へ

オベルネの歴史

オベルネの歴史は紀元前400年頃に始まる。西暦100年頃に町の形態ができ、8世紀頃この地が Obernai (オベルネ)と呼ばれるようになった。その後幾多の変遷を経て、13世紀半端から自由都市として発展してきた。洋菓子においても古い伝統があり、フランス菓子の中でも重要な位置を占めている。

伝統あるオベルネの菓子店の中でも「グロス」は特に高級品の店として知られ、創立以来150年の歴史をもつ。Strasbourg (ストラスブール) で開かれる国際会議における晩餐の

Pâtisserie de l'Alsace de Obernai â Tokyo
アルザスの菓子 オベルネから東京へ

2

3

4

COOKIES

アンテノール
ANTENOR

PL （株）アンテノール企画部
AD （株）アンテノール企画部
D （株）アンテノール企画部

PL Planning Division, Antenor Co., Ltd.
AD Planning Division, Antenor Co., Ltd.
D Planning Division, Antenor Co., Ltd.

1. パンフレット

1. Brochure

1

54

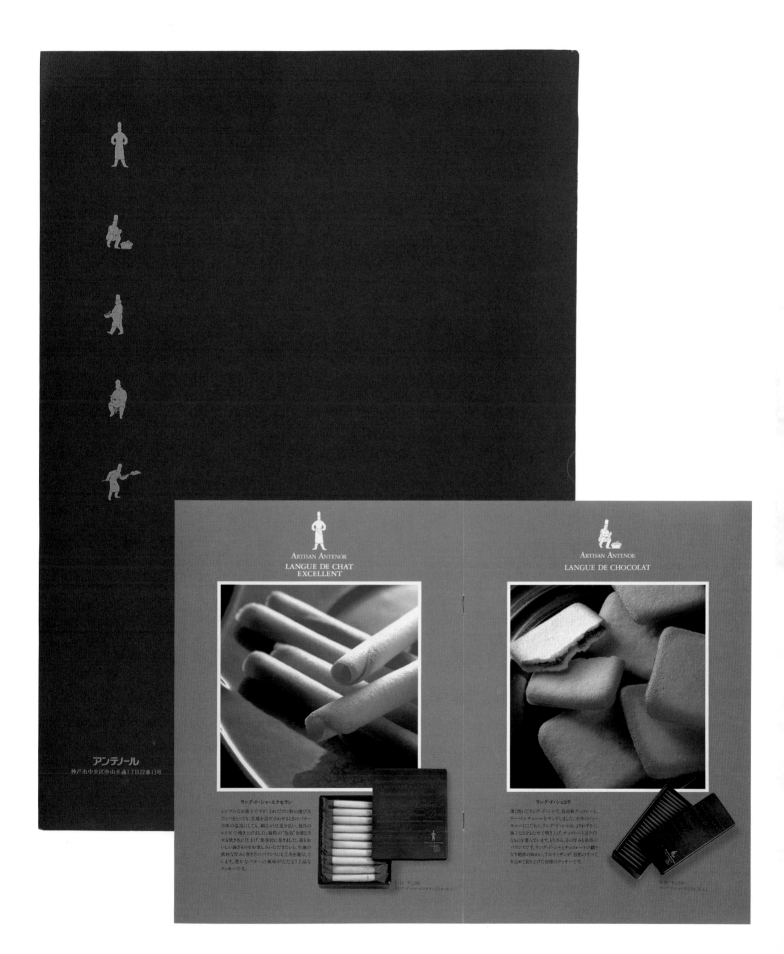

ARTISAN ANTENOR
LANGUE DE CHAT EXCELLENT

ラング・ド・シャ・エクセラン

シンプルなお菓子ですが、それだけに粉の選び方
ひとつをとっても、生地を固ぜ合わせるときのバター
全体の温度にしても、細心の注意を払い、独自の
レシピで焼き上げました。植物の"色気"を感じさ
せる焼き色に仕上げ、美しい形に巻き上げた、格わ
しい歯ざわりをお楽しみいただきたい、生地の
繊妙な甘みと巻き方のバランスにも工夫を凝らして
います。豊かなバターの風味がただよう上品な
クッキーです。

L-12 ¥1,200
ラング・ド・シャ・エクセラン(20本入り)

ARTISAN ANTENOR
LANGUE DE CHOCOLAT

ラング・ド・ショコラ

薄く焼いたラング・ド・シャで、最高級チョコレート、
クーベルチュールをサンドしました。全体のハー
モニーにこだわり、ラング・ド・シャには、ほろ苦さに
耐えさせるために焼き上げ、チョコレートはライト
ないのを選んでいます。もちろん、その旨みも最高の
バランスです。ラング・ド・シャとチョコレートの織り
なす絶妙の味わい、アルティザンが、技術のすべて
を込めて創り上げた自慢のクッキーです。

S-30 ¥1,000
ラング・ド・ショコラ(30本入り)

アンテノール
神戸市中央区中山手通1丁目22番13号

2

3

2. 菓子箱
3. ロゴ

2. Boxes
3. Logotypes

モロゾフ
MOROZOFF

PL　モロゾフ（株）、三浦啓子
AD　（株）商業美術研究所、榎本一弥
D　（株）新生活研究所、藤見恵

PL　Keiko Miura, Morozoff Co., Ltd.
AD　Kazuya Enomoto, Commercial Arts
　　Institute Co., Ltd.
D　Megumi Fujimi, New Lifestyles
　　Institute Co., Ltd.

パンフレット
Brochures

エーデルワイス
EDELWEISS

PL (株)スイス菓子
エーデルワイス企画部
AD (株)スイス菓子
エーデルワイス企画部
D (株)スイス菓子
エーデルワイス企画部

PL Planning Division,
Edelweiss Co., Ltd.
AD Planning Division,
Edelweiss Co., Ltd.
D Planning Division,
Edelweiss Co., Ltd.

パンフレット

Brochures

アンの館
BOUTIQUE DE L'UN

PL （株）アンの館
AD 粟辻アートデレクションルーム
D スタジオ　オオブ

PL Boutique de L'un Co., Ltd.
AD Awatsuji Art Derection Room
D Studio Obu

パンフレット

Brochures

CHOCOLATES

ヴァローナ
VALRHONA

A LA DÉCOUVERTE DU GRAND CHOCOLAT

Vendre la Collection VALRHONA,
c'est initier vos clients au Chocolat Gastronomique.
Faire découvrir au consommateur
le Chocolat des plus Grands Chefs
et des Meilleurs Pâtissiers,
c'est aussi l'habituer à la pâtisserie gastronomique,
vocation des grands artisans du Goût.

VALRHONA

COFFRET COLLECTION 1.2.3

Conçu et dessiné par Sonia Rykiel, ce coffret luxueux permet une dégustation comparative des trois Grands Crus de Chocolat Noir VALRHONA : Guanaja 70 %, Caraïbe 66 % et Manjari 64 %.

Coffret de 3 rangées de 20 carrés de 5 g.

BOÎTE MÉTAL 18 CARRÉS DE GUANAJA 70 %
BOÎTE MÉTAL 18 CARRÉS DE CARAÏBE 66 %

Réinventer le chocolat, comme le fait VALRHONA depuis des années, c'est aussi en repenser la forme et offrir à un chocolat d'exception une boîte métal de présentation originale. Sobre et raffinée elle met parfaitement en valeur les Grands Crus de Chocolat VALRHONA.

Boîtes métal de 18 carrés de 5 g.

EQUINOXE : LA PERLE NOIRE

Equinoxe est une délicate invitation à la gourmandise où s'équilibrent harmonieusement la subtilité tendre des fruits secs et la force du chocolat noir. Sélectionnées parmi les meilleures variétés du monde, les Amandes Marcomas de Catalogne et les Noisettes Romaines d'Italie sont torréfiées à cœur (afin de réveler toutes leurs saveurs fruitées) et laquées de chocolat noir.

Boîte métal de 225 g dans un étui carton.

ÉTUI 4 CARRÉS DE GUANAJA 70 %

Attention raffinée ou plaisir gourmand, cet étui de 4 Carrés de Grand Cru de Chocolat Guanaja permet de déguster à tous moments de la journée la référence du chocolat noir amer.

Étui de 4 carrés de 5 g.

VALRHONA

A LA DÉCOUVERTE DU GRAND CHOCOLAT

Vendre la Collection VALRHONA,
c'est initier vos clients au Chocolat Gastronomique.
Faire découvrir au consommateur
le Chocolat des plus Grands Chefs
et des Meilleurs Pâtissiers,
c'est aussi l'habituer à la pâtisserie gastronomique,
vocation des grands artisans du Goût.

VALRHONA

1

LES FRUITÉS suite

DÉNOMINATION	CARACTÉ-RISTIQUES	DESCRIPTIF	CODE
DOUCE AMANDE	Gamme Noël	Ganache parfumée à l'amande douce, enrobée de chocolat au lait.	
GANACHE CASSIS	Gamme permanente	Ganache à la pulpe de cassis enrobée de chocolat noir.	
GANACHE MANDARINE	Gamme Noël	Ganache réalisée à partir de notre couverture Guanaja, parfumée à la mandarine, enrobée de chocolat noir et présentée sous forme de quartier de mandarine.	
GANACHE POMME	Gamme Noël	Ganache parfumée au Calvados, de forme hexagonale et enrobée de chocolat noir.	
ANIS ÉTOILÉ	Gamme permanente	Ganache intense et rafraîchissante, parfumée à l'essence d'anis étoilé, enrobée de chocolat au lait.	
MENTHE VIVE	Gamme permanente	Ganache intense et rafraîchissante, parfumée à l'essence de menthe vive, enrobée de chocolat noir.	
ORANGETTE	Gamme permanente	Les meilleures origines d'orange d'Espagne confites et enrobées de chocolat noir.	
OTHELLO	Gamme Noël	Ganache à la pulpe de framboise, enrobée de chocolat noir.	
PRALIMINI CITRON	Gamme Noël	Mini-praliné amandes-noisettes parfumé au citron, enrobé de chocolat au lait.	
VALENCIA AMANDE	Gamme permanente	Pâte d'amande, enrobée de chocolat noir, décor amande.	

LES NOUVEAUTÉS NOËL 1994

De nouvelles saveurs, des textures étonnantes, des décors appétissants : tout le savoir-faire de VALRHONA se retrouve dans ces nouveaux bonbons de chocolat.

DÉNOMINATION	CARACTÉ-RISTIQUES	DESCRIPTIF	CODE
LE MÉDITER-RANÉEN	Mendiant	Sur un palet de chocolat issu du mélange subtil de fèves d'origines rares sont délicatement posés des fruits des meilleures origines : écorce d'orange d'Espagne, abricot de Turquie, noisette romaine et pistache sicilienne.	
LE MÉDITER-RANÉEN	Mendiant	Sur un palet de chocolat issu du mélange subtil de fèves d'origines rares sont délicatement posés des fruits des meilleures origines : écorce d'orange d'Espagne, abricot de Turquie, noisette romaine et pistache sicilienne.	
CAISSETTE NOISETTE		Crème de noisettes fondante dressée dans une caissette et décorée d'une noisette italienne vernie.	
RINETTE NOIRE	Praliné	Chocolat entièrement fait à la main, alliant la finesse du praliné et la subtilité du chocolat noir.	
PRALI-FEUILLETÉ	Praliné	Mariage raffiné et croustillant de praliné à base d'amandes d'Espagne et de crêpe dentelle émiettée.	
PRALI-FEUILLETÉ	Praliné	Mariage raffiné et croustillant de praliné à base d'amandes d'Espagne et de crêpe dentelle émiettée.	

CONSEILS DE CONSERVATION DES BONBONS DE CHOCOLAT

- En vitrine à chocolats entre 16° et 16°C.
- % d'humidité de l'air (degré d'hygrométrie) compris entre 55 et 60%.

CONDITIONS DE STOCKAGE DES BOÎTES DE BONBONS DE CHOCOLAT A RÉCEPTION

- Maintenir les boîtes bien fermées au frais (température inférieure à 18°C) et à l'abri de la lumière (celle-ci faisant rancir les matières grasses), les chocolats au lait, noirs, pralinés et décor fruits secs y étant particulièrement sensibles.
- Éviter les chocs thermiques dus à un changement brutal de température entre la pièce de stockage et la vitrine à chocolats. Ces variations subites de température sont à l'origine du blanchiment des chocolats.

LES CAUSES DE BLANCHIMENT

- Le blanchiment gras est dû à une élévation de la température provoquant la fusion des matières grasses. Au bout de quelques jours les matières grasses se recristallisent en surface et donnent un aspect blanchâtre caractéristique.
- Le blanchiment sucré est dû à un environnement très humide ou à la condensation provoquée par une brusque élévation de température.

VALRHONA - 26600 TAIN-L'HERMITAGE - FRANCE   TÉL. 75 07 90 90 - FAX 75 08 05 17 - TÉLEX 346 009 F

BONBONS   SÉLECTION 94/95   CHOCOLAT

Depuis plus de 70 ans, le chocolat VALRHONA est utilisé par les plus Grands Chefs de la gastronomie française.

Tous les talents de VALRHONA se retrouvent dans la gamme de bonbons de chocolat, élaborés à partir des couvertures VALRHONA :

- recherche et sélection des meilleures matières premières,
- recettes respectueuses de la tradition,
- saveurs inimitables et textures onctueuses.

Cette collection, mariage de goûts harmonieux, comblera vos clients amateurs de Grand Chocolat.

LES GANACHES

Les meilleures matières premières ont été utilisées pour réaliser des ganaches tendres et parfumées.

LES GRANDS CRUS

DÉNOMINATION	CARACTÉRISTIQUES	DESCRIPTIF	CODE
GUANAJA AMER	Gamme permanente	Ganache réalisée à partir de notre Grand Cru Guanaja 70% de cacao et enrobée de chocolat noir. Ce chocolat développe en bouche une puissance aromatique extrême.	
GUANAJA LACTÉE	Gamme permanente	Ganache Guanaja Lactée enrobée de chocolat au lait. Ce chocolat marie douceur et amertume.	
CARAÏBE	Gamme permanente	Ganache réalisée à partir de notre Grand Cru Caraïbe et enrobée de chocolat noir.	
MANJARI	Gamme permanente	Ganache réalisée à partir de notre Grand Cru Manjari et enrobée de chocolat noir. Ce chocolat développe en bouche des notes harmonieuses de fruits rouges.	

LES AUTRES GANACHES

DÉNOMINATION	CARACTÉRISTIQUES	DESCRIPTIF	CODE
CAFÉ NOIR	Gamme permanente	Ganache au café arabica, enrobée de chocolat noir et décorée d'un grain de café.	
CAFÉ CRÈME	Gamme permanente	Ganache au café enrobée de couverture Ivoire et décorée d'un grain de café noir.	
PALET OR	Gamme permanente	Un classique réalisé avec une ganache à base de Guanaja 70% de cacao, enrobé de chocolat noir et délicatement doré à la feuille d'or.	
PALET ARGENT	Gamme permanente	Ganache élaborée à partir de notre couverture Équatoriale Lactée, enrobée de chocolat au lait et décorée à la feuille d'argent.	
CHAPKA NOIR	Gamme permanente	Ganache enrobée de chocolat noir et décorée de grains d'amandes Marconas.	
CHAPKA LAIT	Gamme permanente	Ganache au goût subtil de caramel, enrobée de chocolat au lait et décorée de grains d'amandes Marconas.	
JIVARA ALIZÉ	Gamme permanente	Ganache au goût peu sucré aux notes aromatiques de caramel et vanille, enrobée de chocolat au lait.	

LES PRALINÉS

Les meilleures amandes d'Espagne et les inégalables noisettes de Toscane sont grillées à cœur et broyées finement à la meule de pierre selon les méthodes artisanales.

DÉNOMINATION	CARACTÉRISTIQUES	DESCRIPTIF	CODE
CARRÉ PRALINÉ NOIR	Gamme Noël	Praliné aux amandes Valencia, enrobé de chocolat noir et décoré d'une diagonale de chocolat au lait.	
CARRÉ PRALINÉ LAIT	Gamme permanente	Praliné aux amandes Valencia, enrobé de chocolat au lait et décoré d'une diagonale de chocolat noir.	
CARRÉ PRALINÉ IVOIRE	Gamme permanente	Praliné aux amandes Valencia enrobé de chocolat Ivoire et décoré d'une diagonale de chocolat noir.	
EMPIRE NOIR PLIÉ	Gamme Noël	Praliné amandes-noisettes et grains d'amandes Marconas grillées, enrobé de chocolat noir et emballé dans un papier cuivré.	
EMPIRE LAIT PLIÉ	Gamme Noël	Praliné amandes-noisettes et grains d'amandes grillées, enrobé de chocolat au lait et emballé dans un papier doré.	
GRÊTA NOIR	Gamme permanente	Mini-bouchée de praliné amandes-noisettes, enrobée de chocolat noir et décorée de grains d'amandes Marconas.	
GRÊTA LAIT	Gamme permanente	Mini-bouchée de praliné amandes-noisettes enrobée de chocolat au lait et décorée de grains d'amandes Marconas.	
MALAKOFF NOIR	Gamme Noël	Praliné amandes-noisettes enrobé de chocolat noir et décoré de grains d'amandes Marconas.	
MALAKOFF LAIT	Gamme Noël	Praliné amandes-noisettes enrobé de chocolat au lait et décoré d'amandes Marconas.	
NOIX NOIRE	Gamme Noël	Praliné amandes-noisettes dans une coquille moulée de chocolat noir.	
NOIX LAIT	Gamme Noël	Praliné amandes-noisettes et éclats de noix dans une coquille moulée de chocolat au lait.	

LES PRALINÉS suite

DÉNOMINATION	CARACTÉRISTIQUES	DESCRIPTIF	CODE
RINETTE	Gamme permanente	Chocolat fait main, alliant la finesse du praliné aux noisettes romaines et le croquant des grains d'amandes Marconas grillées.	
ÉCUSSON PLIÉ	Gamme Noël	Praliné amandes-noisettes, moulé de chocolat noir, emballé dans un papier doré, bagué de noir et signé d'un écusson.	
BLASON PLIÉ	Gamme Noël	Praliné amandes-noisettes moulé de chocolat au lait, emballé dans un papier doré et décoré d'une bague signée d'un écusson.	
BÛCHETTE	Gamme permanente	Praliné amandes-noisettes dans lequel ont été incorporés des raisins de Corinthe macérés dans du rhum, enrobé de chocolat noir et décoré de paillette de chocolat.	
PRALINOUGAT	Gamme permanente	Praliné amandes-noisettes aux grains de nougat, enrobé de chocolat noir.	
PRALINÉ NOUGATINE	Gamme permanente	Praliné amandes-noisettes aux grains de nougatine croquant enrobé de chocolat au lait.	

LES FRUITÉS

Essences de citron et de menthe, pulpes d'abricot et de framboise, griottes entières et crème de marron, le meilleur des fruits dans le Grand Chocolat.

DÉNOMINATION	CARACTÉRISTIQUES	DESCRIPTIF	CODE
ALICANTE	Gamme permanente	Pâte d'amande pistache enrobée de chocolat noir, décorée d'une pistache.	
CARAFRUTTI ABRICOT	Gamme permanente	Ganache réalisée à partir de Guanaja Lactée et de pulpe d'abricot enrobée de chocolat noir.	
CARAFRUTTI PRUNEAUX	Gamme Noël	Ganache réalisée à partir de Guanaja Lactée et de pulpe de pruneaux caramélisée, enrobée de chocolat noir. Ganache en forme de pruneau.	
CARAFRUTTI COCO	Gamme permanente	Ganache Guanaja Lactée à la pulpe de noix de coco caramélisée et enrobée de chocolat au lait.	
CASTANEA	Gamme Noël	Mélange de fondant et de crème de marron enrobé de chocolat noir, en forme de châtaigne.	

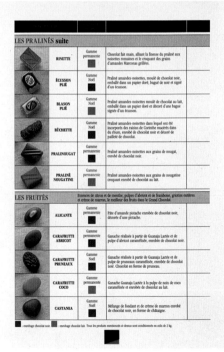

3. 菓子箱、パッケージ
D ソニア・リキエル
3. メタルボックス
AD MBD
D ジャン・クロード・マルバック

3. Boxes, packages
D Sonia Rykiel
3. Cans for chocolates
AD MBD
D Jean-Claude Marbach

4

4. 菓子箱
D ジョエル・デグリップ

4. Boxes
D Joel Desgrippes

5

ノイハウス
NEUHAUS

1. パンフレット
PL 日本ノイハウス（株）
AD 日本ノイハウス（株）
D 包莉

1. Brochures
PL Nihon Neuhaus Co.,Ltd.
AD Nihon Neuhaus Co.,Ltd.
D Bao Ri

1, 3, 4. パッケージ
PL 日本ノイハウス（株）
AD 日本ノイハウス（株）
D 日本ノイハウス（株）

1, 3, 4. Packages
PL Nihon Neuhaus Co., Ltd.
AD Nihon Neuhaus Co., Ltd.
D Nihon Neuhaus Co., Ltd.

2

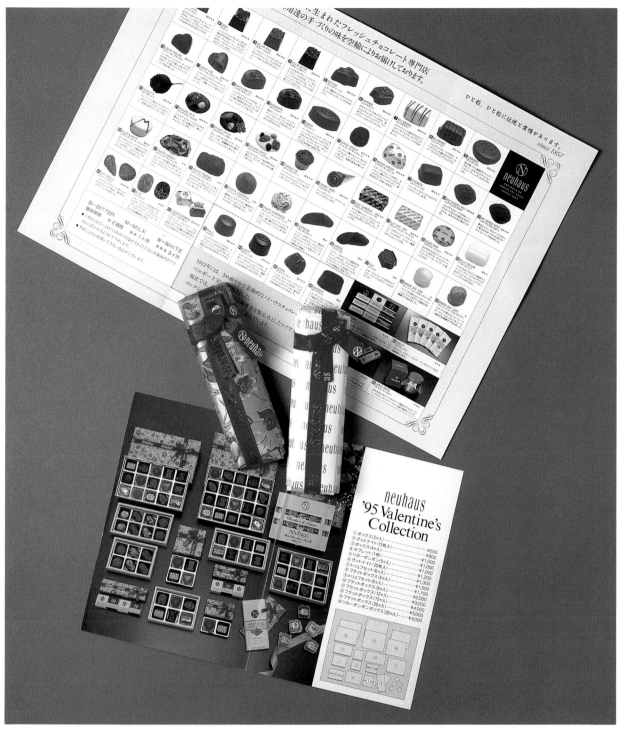

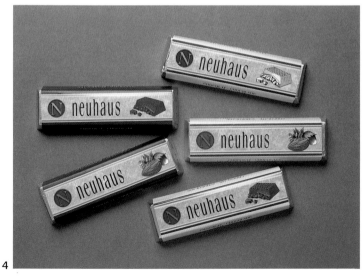

2. パンフレット
3. パンフレット（下）
PL　田島康寛、（株）マック
AD　田島康寛、（株）マック
D　田島康寛、（株）マック

2. Brochures
3. Brochures (bottom)
PL　Yasuhiro Tajima, MAQ Co., Ltd.
AD　Yasuhiro Tajima, MAQ Co., Ltd.
D　Yasuhiro Tajima, MAQ Co., Ltd.

5, 6, 7. パッケージ、包装紙、リボン、
　　　　菓子箱、ショップバッグ
PL　日本ノイハウス（株）
AD　日本ノイハウス（株）
D　　日本ノイハウス（株）

5, 6, 7. Packages, wrapping papers,
　　　　　　streamers, boxes, shopping bags
PL　Nihon Neuhaus Co.,Ltd.
AD　Nihon Neuhaus Co.,Ltd.
D　　Nihon Neuhaus Co.,Ltd.

6

7

コート・ド・フランス
CÔTE DE FRANCE

1. パンフレット
1. Brochures

1, 4, 5. パンフレット
PL サン アンド ドニ(株)、金子誠
AD （株）サンモトヤマ宣伝広報室
D アルゴリズミックアーツ、相馬敏江

1, 4, 5. Brochures
PL Makoto Kaneko, SUN AND DENIS Co., Ltd.
AD Advertising & PR, SUN MOTOYAMA Co., Ltd.
D Toshie Soma, Algorithmic Arts

1. パンフレット

CHOCOLATES

2. 菓子箱
PL　サン アンド ドニ（株）、金子誠
AD　（株）サンモトヤマ宣伝広報室
D　　川路ヨウセイ デザインオフィス、
　　　川路ヨウセイ

2. Boxes
PL　SUN AND DENIS Co., Ltd.
AD　Advertising & PR, SUN
　　　MOTOYAMA Co., Ltd.
D　　Yosei Kawaji, Yosei Kawaji Design
　　　Office

3

3. パンフレット
PL　サン アンド ドニ（株）
AD　（株）サンモトヤマ宣伝広報室
D　（株）コスモ コミュニケーションズ

3. Brochures
PL　SUN AND DENIS Co., Ltd.
AD　Advertising & PR, SUN
　　MOTOYAMA Co., Ltd.
D　Cosmo Communications Co., Ltd.

4

5. 菓子箱
PL コート・ド・フランス社
  フィリップ・ワステルラン

5. Boxes
PL Ph. Wasterlain,
  CÔTE DE FRANCE

BRIDAL GIFT COLLECTION

5

CHOCOLATES

ヴィタメール
WITTAMER

PL （株）ヴィタメールジャポン企画部
AD （株）ヴィタメールジャポン企画部
D （株）ヴィタメールジャポン企画部

PL Planning Division, Wittamer Japon
   Co., Ltd.
AD Planning Division, Wittamer Japon
   Co., Ltd.
D Planning Division, Wittamer Japon
   Co., Ltd.

1. 菓子箱

1. Box

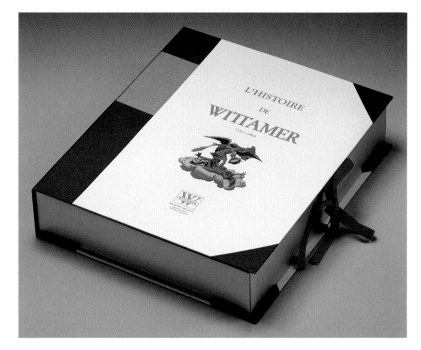

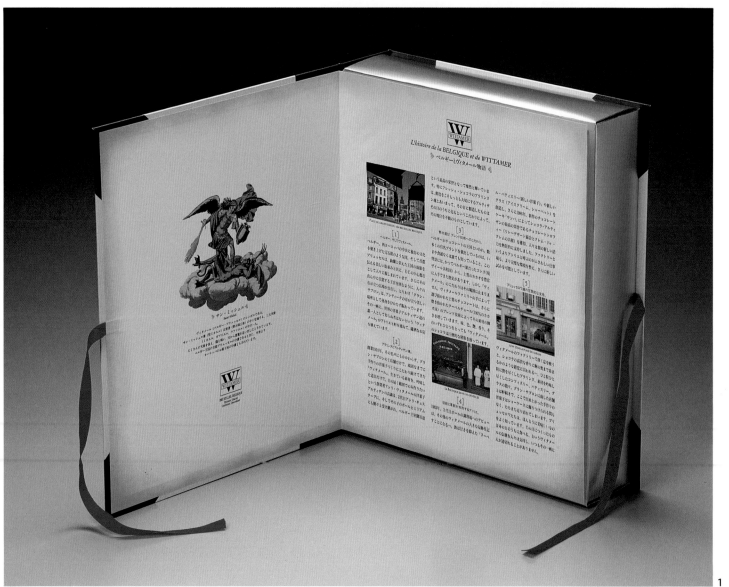

1

Chocolat

Les connaisseurs de chocolats connaissent la différence, l'arôme, ...la subtilité du goût...et ils savent que raffinement n'est possible que s'il y a pureté des produits. L'excellence satisfait le palais et nourrit le coeur. Les chocolats Wittamer faits à la main sont le point culminant de la tradition de la chocolaterie belge par la perfection de leur couleur, saveur, éclat et arôme. Comme les gardes qui protégeaient autrefois leurs chateaux, l'unique magasin Wittamer au Grand Sablon défend l'intégrité de ce métier.

Connoisseurs of our chocolate know the differences, the refined aroma...the luxurious taste...and know that refinement comes only from the purest of ingredients that can be produced. The excellence at once satisfies the palate and nourishes the heart. Handcrafted with unequaled dexterity, Wittamer chocolates climax the tradition of Belgian chocolaterie in perfecting taste, color, shine, and flavor. The chefs of the house were once the sentinels who stood guard in their castle. Like them, the sole Wittamer shop in Grand Sablon, defends the integrity of the trade today.

TRUFFE COGNAC ¥250	TRUFFE KIRCH ¥250	TRUFFE COINTREAU ¥250	TRUFFE SABLON ¥300	TRUFFE CHAMPAGNE ¥250	TRUFFE BLANC ¥230	TRUFFE FONDANT ¥230	TRUFFE MON-BLANC ¥250	TRUFFE LAIT ¥230
CURACAO ¥230	ANANAS ¥230	BLANC ¥230	DIAMANTS ¥230	WITTAMER ¥230	ROSETTE ¥230	VANILLE-FONDANT ¥220	VANILLE-LAIT ¥220	THÉ ¥200
GRENOBLE ¥200	FEUILLE ¥220	COGNAC ¥300	GRAND MARNIER ¥200	MALOU ¥230		AMANDINES ¥180	MENTHE ¥180	CITRON ¥200
COEUR ¥230	PISTACHE ¥220	JAVA ¥180	TRUFFE MAISON PISTACHE ¥230	TRUFFE MAISON AMANDE ¥230				PALAIS OR
DENT DU MIDI ¥220	FAVORITTE ¥180	KIRCH ¥230	CHEVAL-LAIT ¥230	CHEVAL				

W WITTAMER
BRUXELLES, BELGIQUE
Pâtissier, Glacier
Confiseur, Chocolatier

BRUXELLES, BELGIQUE

2

3

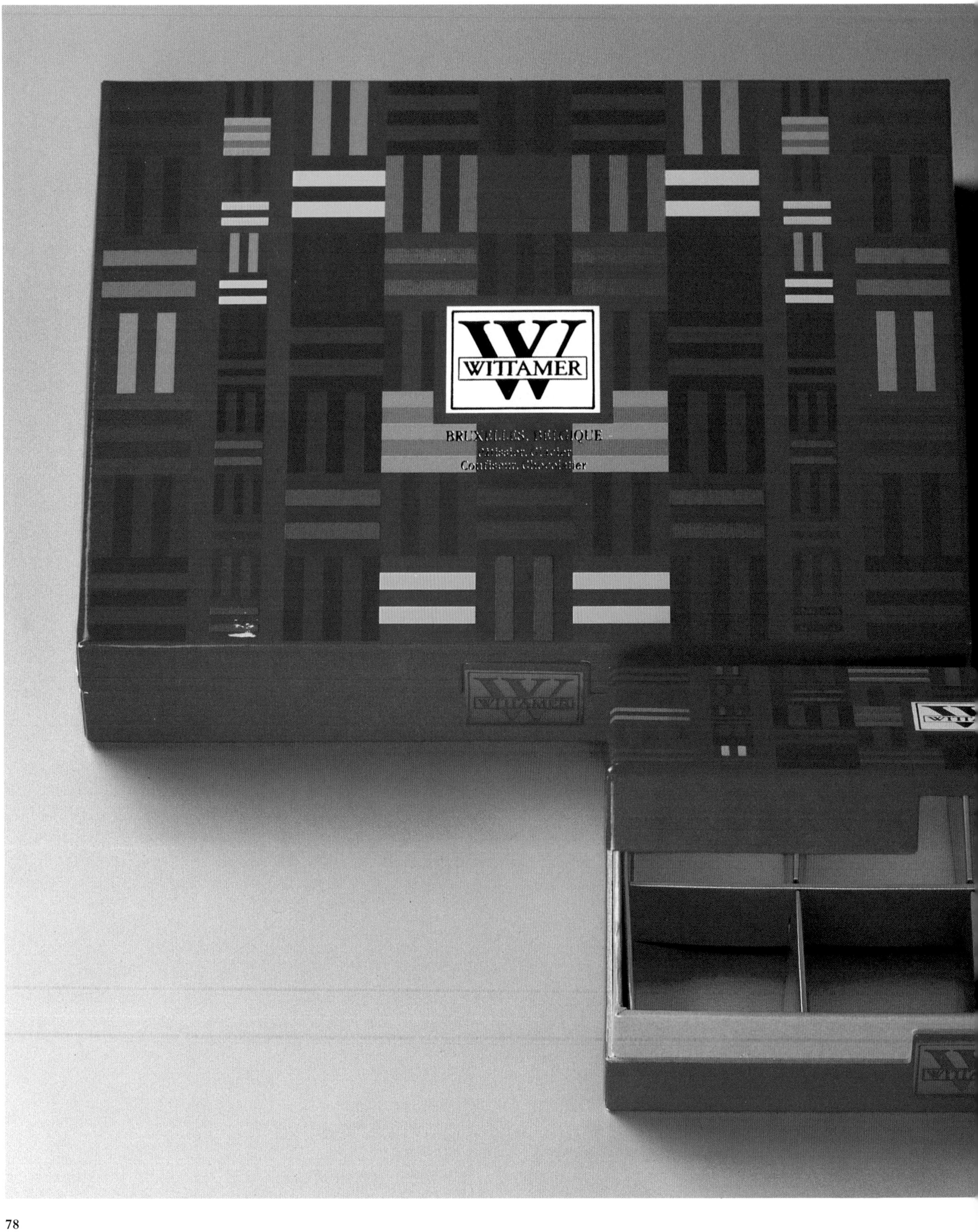
WITTAMER
BRUXELLES, BELGIQUE

5

6

4

メサージュ・ド・ローズ
MESSAGE DE ROSE

PL （株）周プランズワーク
AD 佐藤忠敏
D 　（株）ザ・デザインアソシェイツ

PL Shu Planzwork Co., Ltd.
AD Tadatoshi Sato
D The Design Associates Co., Ltd.

1

1. パンフレット

1. Brochures

2. 菓子箱、包装紙、リボン、封筒

2. Boxes, wrapping paper, ribbon, emvelopes

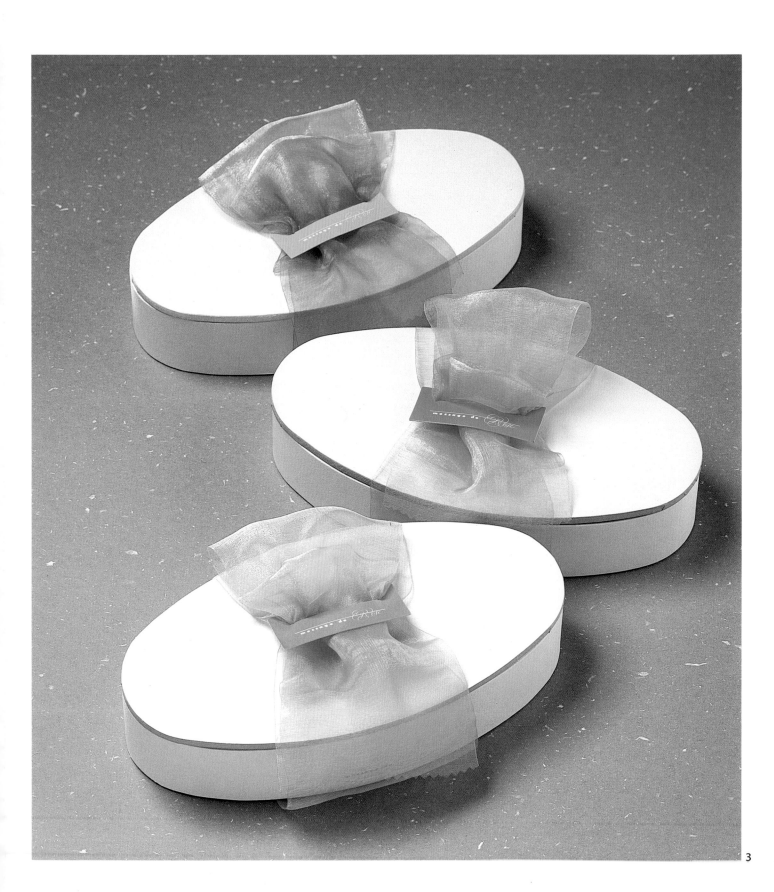

3. 菓子箱、リボン

3. Boxes, ribbbons

エーデルワイス
EDELWEISS

PL （株）スイス菓子エーデルワイス企画部
AD （株）スイス菓子エーデルワイス企画部
D 　（株）スイス菓子エーデルワイス企画部

PL Planning Division, Edelweiss Co., Ltd.
AD Planning Division, Edelweiss Co., Ltd.
D 　Planning Division, Edelweiss Co., Ltd.

パンフレット
Brochure

ゴディバ
GODIVA

1. パンフレット
PL　ゴディバ　ジャパン
AD　（株）博報堂、箭内道彦
D　（株）博報堂、箭内道彦

1. Brochures
PL　GODIVA JAPAN
AD　Michihiko Yanai, HAKUHODO
　　Co., Ltd.
D　Michihiko Yanai, HAKUHODO
　　Co., Ltd.

1

2. バレンタインカタログ
PL　ゴディバ　ジャパン
AD　（株）博報堂、箭内道彦
D　（株）博報堂、箭内道彦

2. Valentine collection
PL　GODIVA JAPAN
AD　Michihiko Yanai, HAKUHODO
　　Co., Ltd.
D　Michihiko Yanai, HAKUHODO
　　Co., Ltd.

2. ギフトカタログ
PL　ゴディバ　ジャパン
AD　（有）千葉デザイン製作所、千葉信敏
D　（有）千葉デザイン製作所、千葉信敏

2. Gift collection
PL　GODIVA JAPAN
AD　Nobutoshi Chiba, Chiba Design
　　Manufacturing Ltd.
D　Nobutoshi Chiba, Chiba Design
　　Manufacturing Ltd.

2

CHOCOLATES

ブールミッシュ
BOUL'MICH

PL （株）ブールミッシュ
AD （株）ブールミッシュ
D　（株）ブールミッシュ

PL　Boul'mich Co., Ltd.
AD　Boul'mich Co., Ltd.
D　 Boul'mich Co., Ltd.

1.パンフレット

1.Brochure

2

3

2. 菓子箱、包装紙
3. パッケージ、菓子箱

2. Box, wrapping paper
3. Packages, boxes

CHOCOLATES

モロゾフ
MOROZOFF

1.パンフレット
PL モロゾフ(株)、構 江美子
AD （株)ヴィイ、林 政司
D （株)ヴィイ、多田裕子

1.Brochures
PL Emiko Kamae, Morozoff Co., Ltd.
AD Masashi Hayashi, VIE Co., Ltd.
D Yuko Tada, VIE Co., Ltd.

2. パッケージ
PL モロゾフ(株)、構 江美子
AD モロゾフ(株)、高橋篤
D モロゾフ(株)、山下真理子、千里プロ
ダクション、吉田健司

2. Packages
PL Emiko Kamae, Morozoff Co., Ltd.
AD Atsushi Takahashi, Morozoff Co.,
Ltd.
D Kenji Yoshida, 1000-Ri Production,
Mariko Yamashita, Morozoff Co.,
Ltd.

1

1

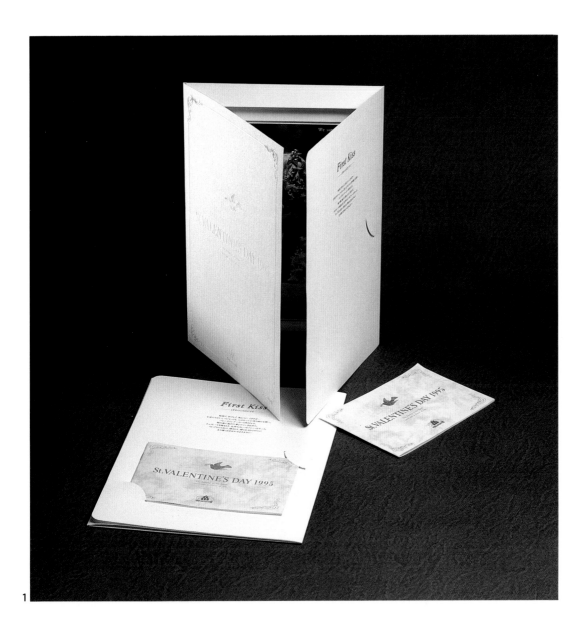

1

2

CHOCOLATES

アンテノール
ANTENOR

PL （株）アンテノール企画部
AD （株）アンテノール企画部
D （株）アンテノール企画部

PL Planning Division, Antenor Co., Ltd.
AD Planning Division, Antenor Co., Ltd.
D Planning Division, Antenor Co., Ltd.

1. パンフレット
2. パンフレット

1. Brochure
2. Brochure

1

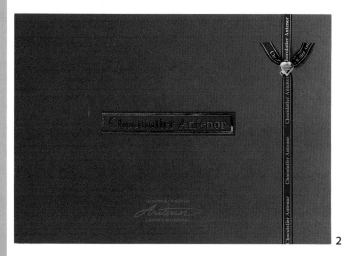

2

ROCHE

胸にハートのメッセージをたずさえてたたずむ、
無邪気で陽気な人形たち。
アンテノールのシェフが一つ一つ、
命をやどすように愛情を込めて削りました。
世界に一つしかない夢のある逸品です。

ロッシェ人形
1個入〈1,500yen〉

ANIMALS

口に入れるのを思わずためらいそうな
ユーモラスで、とても愛らしい動物たち。
夢見る想いを、かわいい人気者の
アニマルチョコレートに託して
心に優しく語りかけます。

アニマル ショコラ
1個入〈350yen〉 2個入〈700yen〉 4個入〈1,400yen〉

1

パンフレット、包装紙
PL ゴンチャロフ製菓（株）企画部
AD ゴンチャロフ製菓（株）企画部
D アトリエ アール、牧江良祐

Brochures,wrapping paper
PL Planning Section, Goncharoff
Confectionery Co., Ltd.
AD Planning Section, Goncharoff
Confectionery Co., Ltd.
D Ryosuke Makie, Atelier R

CHOCOLATES

フーシェ
FOUCHER

PL （株）松風屋
AD （株）松風屋
D （株）デザイン　アイ

PL MATSUKAZEYA Co., Ltd.
AD MATSUKAZEYA Co., Ltd.
D Design Ai Co., Ltd.

パンフレット
Brochures

1. パッケージ、菓子箱
1. Packages, box

PL 六花亭製菓(株)
AD （株）ふきのとう
D （株）ふきのとう

PL Rokkatei Confectionery Co., Ltd.
AD Fukinoto Co., Ltd.
D Fukinoto Co., Ltd.

1

2. パッケージ、絵はがき

2. Packages, postcard

3

3. 菓子箱、パンフレット

3. Boxes, brochures

SWEET VARIETIES

資生堂パーラー
SHISEIDO PARLOUR

1, 2. パンフレット
PL （株）資生堂パーラー
AD （株）資生堂宣伝部、村井和章
D （株）資生堂宣伝部、村井和章、

1, 2. Brochures
PL SHISEIDO PARLOUR Co., Ltd.
AD Kazuaki Murai, Advertising Division,
   SHISEIDO Co., Ltd.
D Kazuaki Murai, Advertising Division,
   SHISEIDO Co., Ltd.

1

2

3

3. 包装紙、リボン

3. Wrapping paper, streamer

4

4.5. 菓子箱
PL （株）資生堂パーラー
AD 仲條正義、三宅章夫
D 仲條正義、三宅章夫、山田尊康

4.5. Boxes
PL SHISEIDO PARLOUR Co., Ltd.
AD Masayoshi Nakajo, Akio Miyake
D Masayoshi Nakajo, Akio Miyake,
Takayasu Yamada

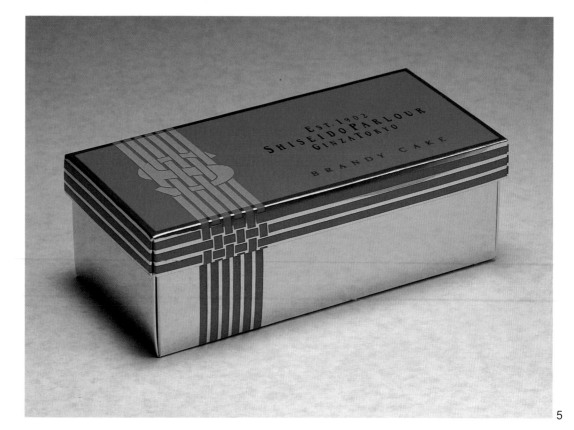

5

6

6. ショップバッグ、シール

6. Shopping bag, seals

7. パンフレット
PL （株）資生堂パーラー
AD （株）資生堂宣伝部、村井和章
D （株）資生堂宣伝部、村井和章

7. Brochures
PL SHISEIDO PARLOUR Co., Ltd.
AD Kazuaki Murai , Advertising Division,
    SHISEIDO Co., Ltd.
D Kazuaki Murai , Advertising Division,
    SHISEIDO Co., Ltd.

7

8. 菓子箱、パッケージ
PL （株）資生堂パーラー
AD 仲條正義
D 仲條正義

8. Box, packages
PL SHISEIDO PARLOUR Co., Ltd.
AD Masayoshi Nakajo
D Masayoshi Nakajo

8

1

1. パンフレット
PL （有）ビジュアルクリエイト、斉藤秀夫
AD （有）アドバタイジング　ストア、彦山敦
D 　（有）アドバタイジング　ストア、長谷川知子

1. Brochures
PL Hideo Saito, VISUAL CREATE Co., Ltd.
AD Atsushi Hikoyama, AD Store Co., Ltd.
D 　Tomoko Hasegawa, AD store Co., Ltd.

1. 菓子箱
PL （株）グラディア、大橋進
AD （株）グラディア、大橋進
D 　（株）グラディア、井上隆、上田姫美、工藤聡

1. Boxes
PL Susumu Ohasi, GRADIA Co., Ltd.
AD Susumu Ohasi, GRADIA Co., Ltd.
D 　Takashi Inoue, Kimi Ueda, Satoru
　　Kudo, GRADIA Co., Ltd.

2

3

2, 3. 菓子箱
PL （株）グラディア、大橋進
AD （株）グラディア、大橋進
D （株）グラディア、井上隆、上田姫美、工藤聡

2, 3. Boxes
PL Susumu Ohasi, GRADIA Co., Ltd.
AD Susumu Ohasi, GRADIA Co., Ltd.
D Takashi Inoue, Kimi Ueda, Satoru
Kudo, GRADIA Co., Ltd.

SWEET VARIETIES

ペルティエ
PELTIER

PL ユーハイム企画室
AD ユーハイム企画室
D ユーハイム企画室

PL Juchheim's Planning Office
AD Juchheim's Planning Office
D Juchheim's Planning Office

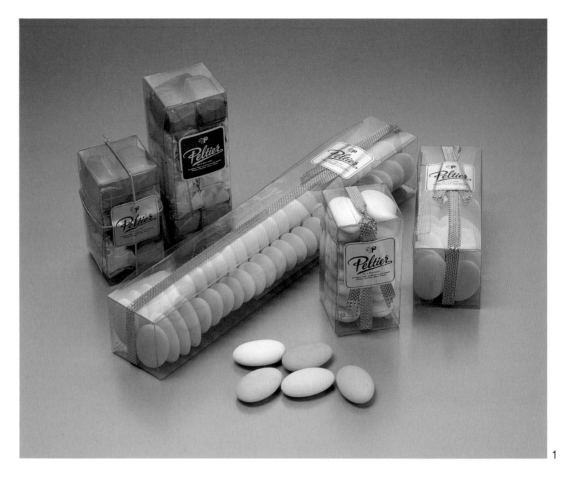

1. パッケージ
2. パンフレット

1. Packages
2. Brochures

1

2

3

4

4. 菓子箱、パッケージ、包装紙
5. 菓子箱

4. Box, packages, wrapping paper
5. Box

5

SWEET VARIETIES

ダロワイヨ
DALLOYAU

PL （株）ダロワイヨジャポン
AD （株）ダロワイヨジャポン
D （株）カワサキデザインオフィス

PL DALLOYAU JAPON Co., Ltd.
AD DALLOYAU JAPON Co., Ltd.
D Kawasaki Design Office Co., Ltd.

1

1. パンフレット

1. Brochures

2

2. パンフレット、菓子箱、包装紙、リボン

2. Brochure, box, wrapping paper, streamer

3. 菓子箱、パッケージ

3. Boxes, packages

SWEET VARIETIES

和光
WAKO

1. パンフレット
PL 大日本印刷（株）
AD （株）和光
D 大日本印刷（株）CDC事業部

1.Brochures
PL Dai-Nippon Printing Co.,Ltd.
AD Wako Co., Ltd.
D Creative Design Center Devision,
Dai-Nippon Printing Co.,Ltd.

1

2

2. 菓子箱
PL （株）和光、木谷明子
AD （株）和光、木谷明子
D （株）ジー・アンド・エー、島田ゆり子

2. Boxes
PL Akiko Kitani, Wako Co., Ltd.
AD Akiko Kitani, Wako Co., Ltd.
D   Yuriko Shimada, G&A Co., Ltd.

3

3. 菓子箱
PL （株）和光、木谷明子
AD （株）和光、木谷明子
D 箱、木谷明子
　　帯、島田ゆり子

3. Boxes
PL Akiko Kitani, Wako Co., Ltd.
AD Akiko Kitani, Wako Co., Ltd.
D Box, Akiko Kitani
　　Streamer, Yuriko Shimada

4. 菓子箱
PL （株）和光、木谷明子
AD （株）和光、木谷明子
D （株）ジー・アンド・エー、島田ゆり子

4. Boxes
PL Akiko Kitani, Wako Co., Ltd.
AD Akiko Kitani, Wako Co., Ltd.
D Yuriko Shimada, G&A Co., Ltd.

4

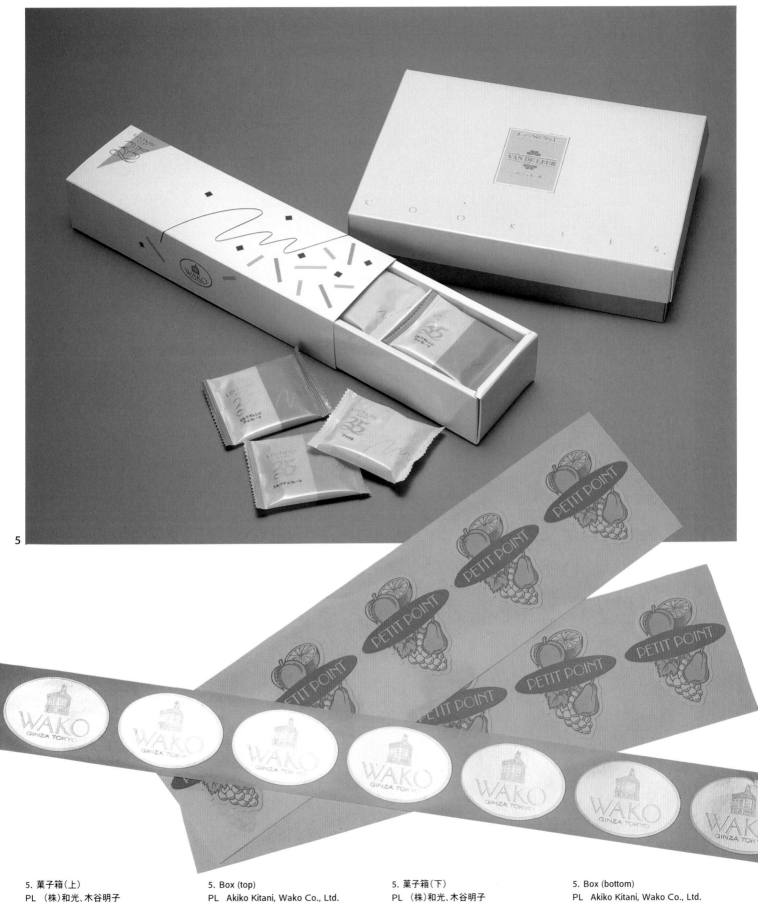

5. 菓子箱（上）
PL （株）和光、木谷明子
AD （株）和光、木谷明子
D （株）ジー・アンド・エー、島田ゆり子

5. Box (top)
PL Akiko Kitani, Wako Co., Ltd.
AD Akiko Kitani, Wako Co., Ltd.
D Yuriko Shimada, G&A Co., Ltd.

5. 菓子箱（下）
PL （株）和光、木谷明子
AD （株）和光、木谷明子
D （株）ジー・アンド・エー、浅沼　剛

5. Box (bottom)
PL Akiko Kitani, Wako Co., Ltd.
AD Akiko Kitani, Wako Co., Ltd.
D Go Asanuma, G&A Co., Ltd.

SWEET VARIETIES

ロイスダール
LOISDAR

1,2,3,4 パンフレット
PL （株）ナックス、斉藤康子
D （株）パウダースノー、池田博範

1,2,3,4. Brochures
PL Yasuko Saito, Nax Co., Ltd.
D Hironori Ikeda, Powder Snow Co., Ltd.

1

2

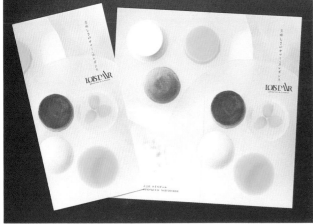

3. 菓子箱
D 企画工房、上村昭二

3. Box
D Shoji Kamimura, Kikaku Kobo

5. 菓子箱
5. Boxes

6

5. 菓子箱
6. パッケージ
D 企画工房、上村昭二

5. Boxes
6. Packages
D Shoji Kamimura,Kikaku Kobo

SWEET VARIETIES

ヨックモック
YOKU MOKU

1. パンフレット
PL （株）ヨックモック
AD 大森幸代（バンケット）
D 大森幸代（バンケット）

1. Brochures
PL YOKU MOKU Co.,Ltd.
AD Yukiyo Omori (Banquet)
D Yukiyo Omori (Banquet)

1

2

2. 缶
PL 近藤司
AD 松原章二
D 川路ヨウセイ
2. Cans for cookies
PL Tsukasa Kondo
AD Shoji Matsubara
D Yosei Kawaji

3, 4. パンフレット
PL （株）ヨックモック
AD 大森幸代（バンケット）
D 大森幸代（バンケット）

3, 4. Brochures
PL YOKU MOKU Co.,Ltd.
AD Yukiyo Omori (Banquet)
D Yukiyo Omori (Banquet)

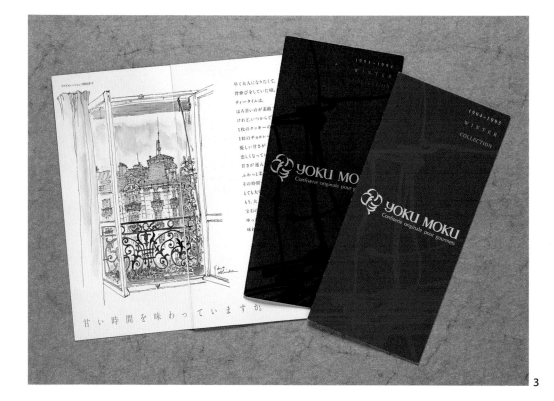

3

ふりむけば、
ありがとうの
顔がある。
お歳暮に、ヨックモック。

冬の足音が近づいてくると、

なぜか思い出す笑顔があります。

あの方のあれこれを思い浮かべるたびに、

胸の奥があたたかくなるのはなぜでしょう。

冬のひかりのリボンをかけて、

あなたに届ける「ありがとう」…。

今年も優しい響きでありますように。

ヨックモックのお歳暮です。

4

5

5. 缶
PL 近藤司
AD 松原章二
D 川路ヨウセイ

5. Cans for cookies
PL Tsukasa Kondo
AD Shoji Matsubara
D Yosei Kawaji

ぶどうの木
BUDO-NO-KI

1

1. パンフレット、菓子箱、パッケージ
PL （株）グレープストーン・菓子企画部
AD （株）ミックブレインセンター
D （株）ミックブレインセンター

1. Brochures, boxes, packages
PL Grape Stone Co., Ltd.
AD MIC Brain Center Co., Ltd.
D MIC Brain Center Co., Ltd.

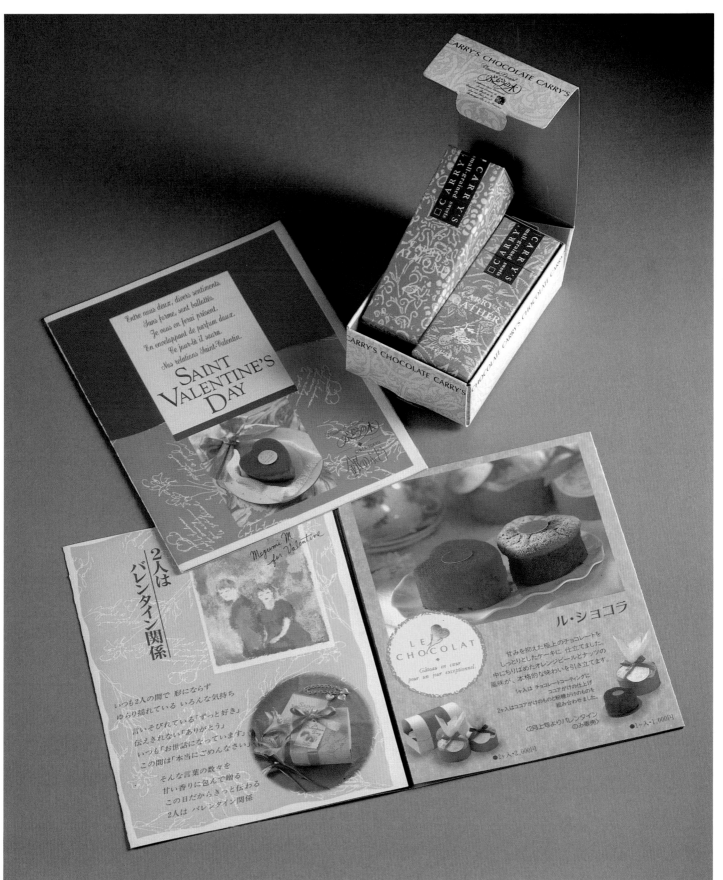

2

2. パンフレット
PL （株）グレープストーン・菓子企画部
AD （株）グレープストーン・菓子企画部
D　（株）グレープストーン・菓子企画部

2. Brochures
PL　Grape Stone Co., Ltd.
AD　Grape Stone Co., Ltd.
D　　Grape Stone Co., Ltd.

2. 菓子箱
PL （株）グレープストーン・菓子企画部
AD （株）ミックブレインセンター
D　（株）ミックブレインセンター

2. Boxes
PL　Grape Stone Co., Ltd.
AD　MIC Brain Center Co., Ltd.
D　　MIC Brain Center Co., Ltd.

3. パンフレット
PL （株）グレープストーン・菓子企画部
AD （株）グレープストーン・菓子企画部
D （株）グレープストーン・菓子企画部
4. パンフレット
PL （株）グレープストーン・菓子企画部
AD （株）ミックブレインセンター
D （株）ミックブレインセンター

3.Brochures
PL Grape Stone Co., Ltd.
AD Grape Stone Co., Ltd.
D Grape Stone Co., Ltd.
4. Brochures
PL Grape Stone Co., Ltd.
AD MIC Brain Center Co., Ltd.
D MIC Brain Center Co., Ltd.

3

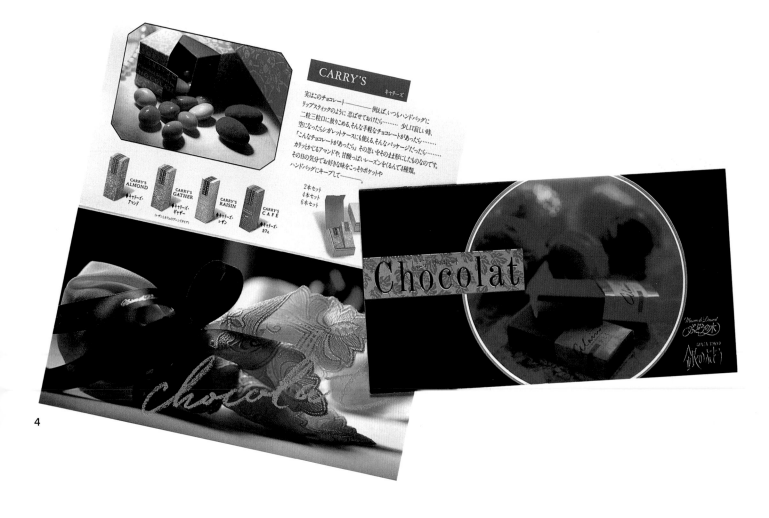

4

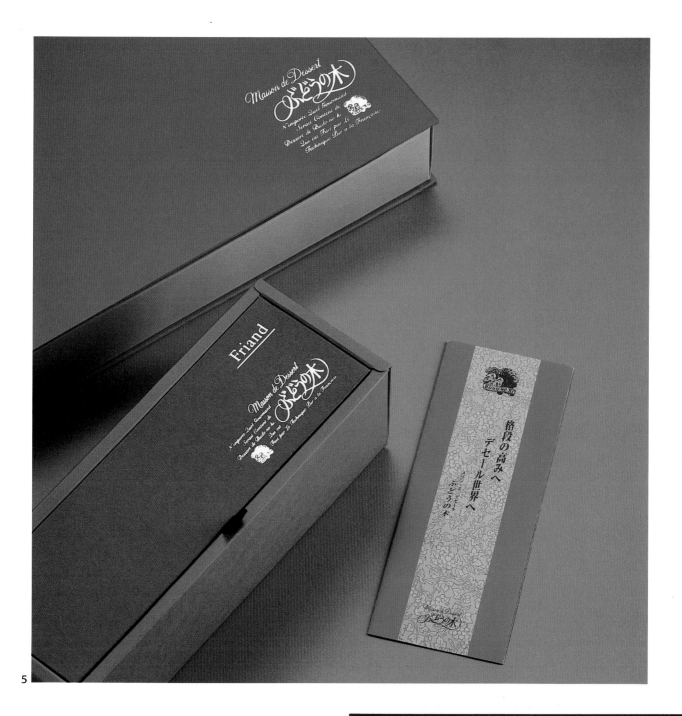

5. パンフレット、菓子箱
6. パンフレット
PL （株）グレープストーン・菓子企画部
AD （株）ミックブレインセンター
D （株）ミックブレインセンター

5. Brochure, boxes
6. Brochure
PL Grape Stone Co., Ltd.
AD MIC Brain Center Co., Ltd.
D MIC Brain Center Co., Ltd.

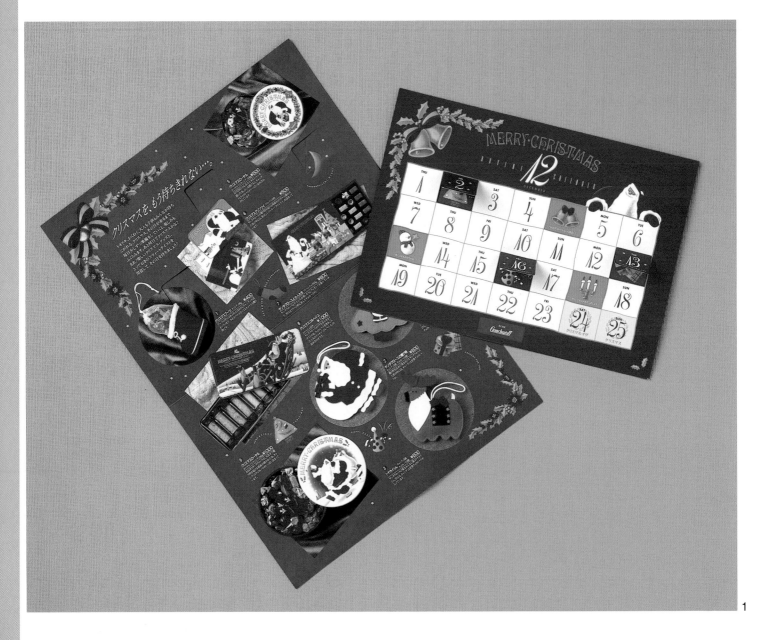

1

2

1. カレンダー
PL ゴンチャロフ製菓(株)企画部
AD ゴンチャロフ製菓(株)企画部
D (株)アッシュ

1. Calender
PL Planning Section, Goncharoff
Confectionery Co., Ltd.
AD Planning Section,Goncharoff
Confectionery Co., Ltd.
D Ashe Co., Ltd.

2. 菓子箱、シール
2. Box, seals

3

3. ショップバッグ、包装紙、菓子箱
PL　ゴンチャロフ製菓(株)企画部
AD　ゴンチャロフ製菓(株)企画部
D　　アトリエ アール、牧江良祐

3. Shopping bags, wrapping paper, box
PL　Planning Section, Goncharoff
　　 Confectionery Co., Ltd.
AD　Planning Section, Goncharoff
　　 Confectionery Co., Ltd.
D　　Ryosuke Makie, Atelie R

4. パンフレット、菓子缶
PL ゴンチャロフ製菓(株)企画部
AD ゴンチャロフ製菓(株)企画部
D アトリエ アール、牧江良祐

4. Brochures, cans for candies
PL Planning Section, Goncharoff
   Confectionery Co., Ltd.
AD Planning Section, Goncharoff
   Confectionery Co., Ltd.
D Ryosuke Makie, Atelie R

クローバー
CLOVER

PL （株）ふらんす菓子　クローバー
AD （株）ふらんす菓子　クローバー
D　（株）ふらんす菓子　クローバー

PL　CLOVER Co., Ltd.
AD　CLOVER Co., Ltd.
D　CLOVER Co., Ltd.

1. パンフレット、リーフレット

1. Brochure, leaflets

1

2. パンフレット、菓子箱

2. Brochure、box

3

SWEET VARIETIES

不二家
FUJIYA

PL 日本サンフィルム、
   阿部博デザイン事務所
PD 佐々木健二
AD 阿部博
D 山崎里香
PH 植野淳
ST 佐藤恭子
IL 中沢由美子

PL Hiroshi Abe Design Division Office,
   Nippon Sun Film
PD Kenji Sasaki
AD Hiroshi Abe
D Rika Yamazaki
PH Jun Ueno
ST Kyoko Sato
IL Yumiko Nakazawa

1. パンフレット

1. Brochures

2

パティスリー・ラ・マーレ・ド・チャヤ
（日影茶屋）

LES PATISSERIES LA MARÉE DE CHAYA (HIKAGE CHAYA)

PL （株）チャヤレストランシステムズ,
　　宮本修
AD （株）チャヤレストランシステムズ,
　　宮本修
D 　（株）チャヤレストランシステムズ,
　　宮本修

PL Osamu Miyamoto, Chaya
　　Restaurant Systems Co., Ltd.
AD Osamu Miyamoto, Chaya
　　Restaurant Systems Co., Ltd.
D 　Osamu Miyamoto, Chaya
　　Restaurant Systems Co., Ltd.

1. パンフレット

1. Brochures

菓子舖
日影茶屋

〖節句菓子〗

古くからその節にまつわるいわれ。
季節が待ちどおしくなるような楽しみのお菓子。
伝統行事に欠かせないお菓子をお作りし、
皆様の追儺と益々のご健勝をお祈り申し上げます。

人日の節供（葩餅）
桃の節供（ひちぎり）
端午の節供（茅巻・柏餅）
七夕の節供（短丹薯蕷）
重陽の節供（菊景色）
節分（うぐいす餅、益豆）

節供当日迄の三日間の限定販売とさせて頂きます。

化粧箱入り　一、八〇〇円

四季を映したお菓子。
その季節に最もふさわしくなじみの深いものを
上品に仕上げております。

うぐいす餅（二月一日〜三日）
わらび餅（二月、三月）
おはぎ（春・秋・お彼岸）
麩饅頭（六月〜八月）
水羊羹（七月、八月）
栗茶巾絞り（十月、十一月）

数に限りがございます。ご予約も承ります。
歳時により、価格が異なります。

SWEET VARIETIES

ブールミッシュ
BOUL'MICH

PL （株）ブールミッシュ
AD （株）ブールミッシュ
D （株）ブールミッシュ

PL Boul'mich Co., Ltd.
AD Boul'mich Co., Ltd.
D Boul'mich Co., Ltd.

1

2

1, 2. パンフレット

1, 2. Brochures

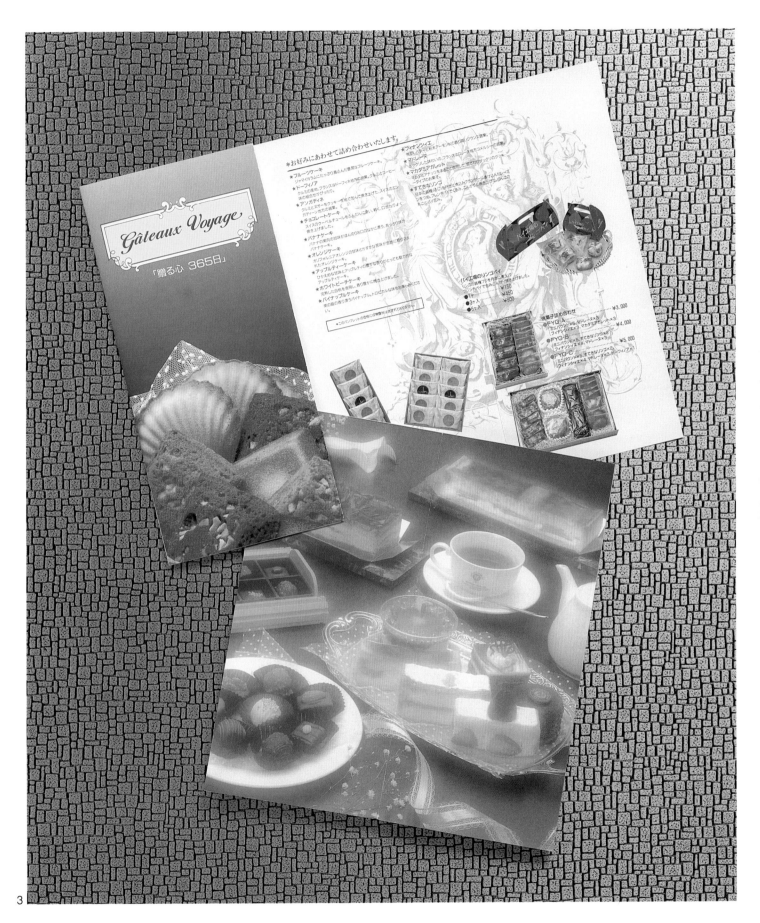

3

SWEET VARIETIES

クレッセント
CRESCENT

PL （株）クレッセント、柳正司
AD （株）クレッセント、柳正司
D （株）クレッセント、柳正司

PL　Tadashi Yanagi, Crescent Co., Ltd.
AD　Tadashi Yanagi, Crescent Co., Ltd.
D　 Tadashi Yanagi, Crescent Co., Ltd.

パンフレット		Brochures	
PL	（株）コミュニケーション・メントース、比地修	PL	Osamu Hiji, Communication Mentors Co., Ltd.
AD	（株）コミュニケーション・メントース、比地修	AD	Osamu Hiji, Communication Mentors Co., Ltd.
D	（株）コミュニケーション・メントース、比地修	D	Osamu Hiji, Communication Mentors Co., Ltd.

SWEET VARIETIES

エーデルワイス
EDELWEISS

PL (株)スイス菓子エーデルワイス企画部
AD (株)スイス菓子エーデルワイス企画部
D (株)スイス菓子エーデルワイス企画部

PL Planning Division, Edelweiss Co., Ltd.
AD Planning Division, Edelweiss Co., Ltd.
D Planning Division, Edelweiss Co., Ltd.

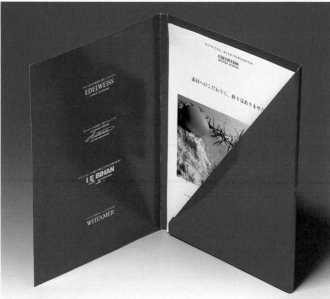

パンフレット

Brochures

パンフレット
PL （株）アドブレイクス
AD （有）テンポイントスタジオ
D （有）テンポイントスタジオ

Brochures
PL AD Breaks Co., Ltd.
AD Ten Point Studio Ltd.
D Ten Point Studio Ltd.

SWEET VARIETIES

フーシェ
FOUCHER

PL （株）松風屋
AD （株）松風屋
D （株）デザイン　アイ

PL Matsukazeya Co., Ltd.
AD Matsukazeya Co., Ltd.
D Design Ai Co., Ltd.

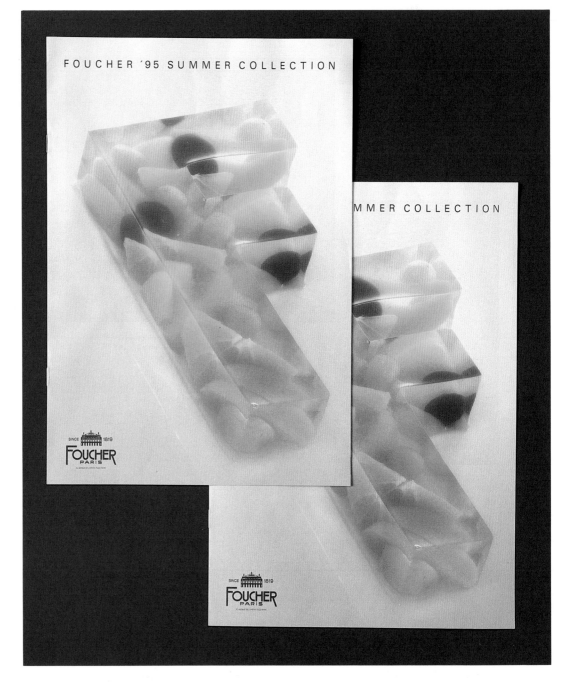

パンフレット
Brochures

パンフレット
PL　（株）三旺物産
AD　新磯信一郎
D　　新磯信一郎

包装紙、菓子箱、リボン
PL　（株）三旺物産
AD　（株）フリップサイドコレクション
D　　（株）ブーベ

Brochure
PL　Sanoh Bussan Co., Ltd.
AD　Shinichiro Niiso
D　　Shinichiro Niiso

Wrapping papers, box, streamer
PL　Sanoh Bussan Co., Ltd.
AD　Flip Side Collection Co., Ltd.
D　　Bouve Co., Ltd.

明治製菓
MEIJI SEIKA

1. パンフレット、パッケージ
PL　明治製菓（株）
AD　亀倉雄策
D　亀倉雄策

1. Brochure, packages
PL　Meiji Seika Co., Ltd.
AD　Yusaku Kamekura
D　Yusaku Kamekura

1

2. パンフレット、菓子箱
PL トッパン パッケージ センター、明治製菓(株)
AD トッパン パッケージ センター、明治製菓(株)
D トッパン パッケージ センター、明治製菓(株)

2. Brochure, boxes
PL Toppan Packaging Center,Meiji Seika Co., Ltd.
AD Toppan Packaging Center,Meiji Seika Co., Ltd.
D Toppan Packaging Center,Meiji Seika Co., Ltd.

2

3

3.パッケージ
PL 明治製菓(株)、大日本印刷(株)包装
   総合開発センター
AD 明治製菓(株)、大日本印刷(株)包装
   総合開発センター
D 友廣謙一、春木敏雄、柳田京三

3. Packages
PL Meiji Seika Co., Ltd., Package
   Planning Div. Dainippon Printing
   Co., Ltd.
AD Meiji Seika Co., Ltd., Package
   Planning Div. Dainippon Printing
   Co., Ltd.
D Kenichi Tomohiro, Toshio Haruki,
   Kyozo Yanagida

雪印乳業
SNOW BRAND MILK PRODUCTS

AD 雪印乳業（株）宣伝部
AD Advertising Dept., Snow Brand Milk Products Co., Ltd.

1

1. 商品カタログ

1. Product catalogs

2

菓子箱（左）
D 大日本印刷（株）PAC

Box(left)
D PAC, Dainippon Printing Co., Ltd.

菓子箱（中）
D （株）ミツモト

Box(center)
D Mitsumoto Co., Ltd.

菓子箱（右）
D （株）YAO デザインインターナショナル

Box(right)
D Yao Design International Co., Ltd.

パッケージ（カップ）
D （株）YAO デザインインターナショナル

Packages(cups)
D Yao Design International Co., Ltd.

パッケージ（上、中）
D （株）YAO デザインインターナショナル

Packages(top,middle)
D Yao Design International Co., Ltd.

パッケージ（下）
D 凸版印刷（株）TPC

Package(bottom)
D TPC, Toppan Printing Co., Ltd.

森永製菓
MORINAGA & CO., LTD.

1. 商品カタログ
PL 福田秀一
AD 奥山　高
D 柳川峻明

1. Product catalogs
PL Syuichi Hukuda
AD Takasi Okuyama
D Takaaki Yanagawa

2. 商品カタログ
PL 山本健二
AD 奥山　高
D 須山一彦

2. Product catalogs
PL Kenji Yamamoto
AD Takashi Okuyama
D Kazuhiko Suyama

1

2

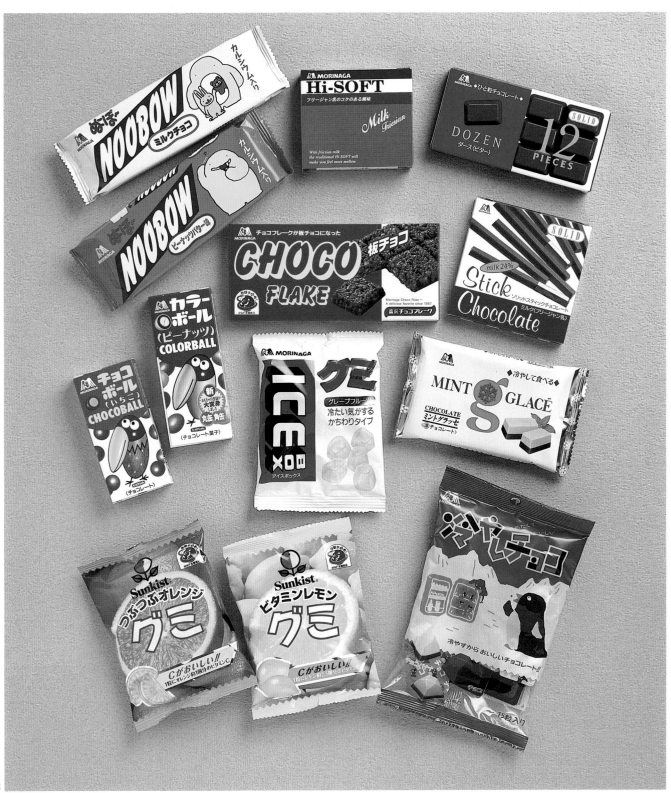

3

小岩井乳業
KOIWAI DAIRY PRODUCTS

1, 2. 菓子箱、パッケージ
D　（株）PAOS デザイン研究所

1, 2. Box, packages
D　PAOS Co., Ltd.

1

2

JAPNESE CONFECTIONERIES

和菓子

鎌倉へようこそ

鎌倉が「鎌倉」である限り人々は遥か未来の歴史の再生を夢見、悠々とした歴史のある人々が健在であることの証しのようにみえます。それはどのような破壊よりも、どのように壮大な建設よりも、はるかに多くの困難に充ちていました。手を触れぬまま遺し置いたのでした。

うらうらと陽だまりの香りが匂い立つのは、知恵や勇気のある人々が健在であることの証しのあかしのようにみえます。

滅すことで歴史を進めたこの国の、ここだけには、人々は時代の翼を左げて眠る島のようにとおしさを覚え、信じることができるのです。

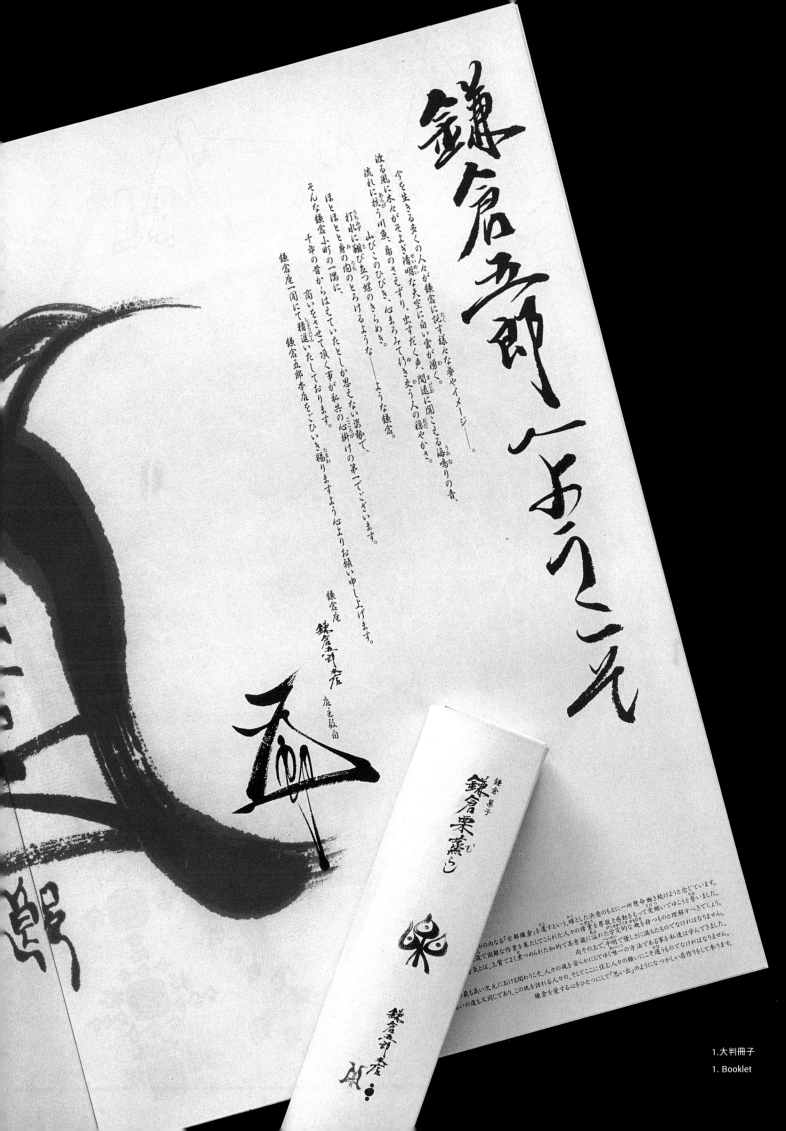

鎌倉五郎へあうて兄

今を生きる多くの人々が鎌倉に託す様々な夢やイメージ——。
渡る風に木々がそよぎ清洌な天空に白い雲が湧く。
流れに抗う川魚、鳥のさえずり、遠すたく声、間遠に聞こえる海鳴りの音、
山びこのひびき、出まろみて行き交う人の穏やかさ。——ような鎌倉。
打水に翔び立つ蝶のきらめき、身の肉のとろけるような
ほとほとと、こんな鎌倉小町の一隅に、
千年の昔からはえていたとしか思えない激動で、
商いをさせて頂く事が私共の心掛けの第一でございます。
鎌倉店一同にて精進いたしております。
鎌倉五郎本店をどひいき賜りますよう心よりお願い申し上げます。

鎌倉店
鎌倉五郎本店
店主敬白

鎌倉菓子
鎌倉栗蒸し

鎌倉五郎本店

1. 大判冊子
PL （株）鎌倉座　企画部
AD （株）ミックブレインセンター
D （株）ミックブレインセンター

1. Booklet
PL Kamakura-za Co., Ltd.
AD Mic Brain Center Co., Ltd.
D Mic Brain Center Co., Ltd.

1

1

1

2

2. パンフレット（右）　　　　　　　　2. Brochures (right)
PL　（株）鎌倉座　企画部　　　　　　PL　Kamakura-za Co., Ltd.
AD　（株）鎌倉座　企画部　　　　　　AD　Kamakura-za Co., Ltd.
D　（株）鎌倉座　企画部　　　　　　　D　Kamakura-za Co., Ltd.
2. パンフレット（左）、菓子箱　　　　2. Brochure (left), boxes
PL　（株）鎌倉座　企画部　　　　　　PL　Kamakura-za Co., Ltd.
AD　（株）ミックブレインセンター　　AD　MIC Brain Center Co., Ltd.
D　（株）ミックブレインセンター　　　D　MIC Brain Center Co., Ltd.

無汸庵
MUHOAN

1

PL　綿貫宏介
AD　綿貫宏介
D　　綿貫宏介

PL　Hirosuke Watanuki
AD　Hirosuke Watanuki
D　　Hirosuke Watanuki

1. 小冊子

1. Booklet

2

2. 封筒、便せん、菓子箱

2. Stationery, box

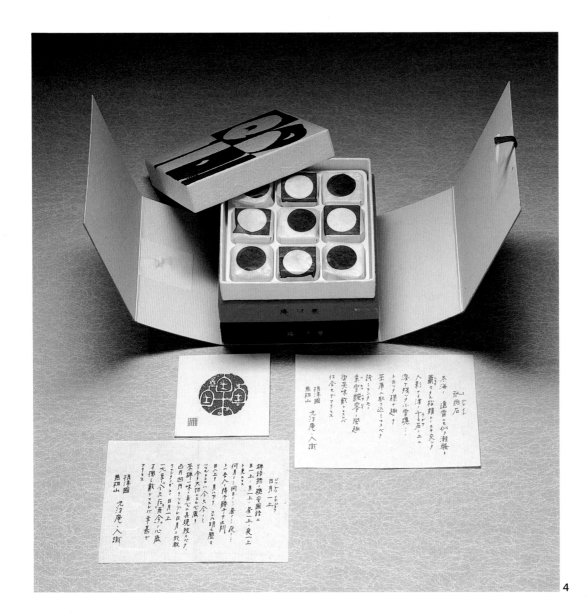

4

5

6

7. 菓子箱
7. Boxes

仙太郎
SENTARO

PL　仙太郎(株)、田中護
AD　仙太郎(株)、田中護
D　　仙太郎(株)、田中護

PL　Mamoru Tanaka, Sentaro Co., Ltd.
AD　Mamoru Tanaka, Sentaro Co., Ltd.
D　　Mamoru Tanaka, Sentaro Co., Ltd.

JAPANESE SWEETS

鶴屋吉信
TURUYA-YOSHINOBU

PL 鶴屋吉信　営業企画
AD 鶴屋吉信　営業企画
D 鶴屋吉信　営業企画

PL Turuya-Yoshinobu Business
   Planning Department
AD Turuya-Yoshinobu Business
   Planning Department
D Turuya-Yoshinobu Business
   Planning Department

1. パンフレット
1. Brochures

2. 菓子箱
2. Box

3. 菓子箱

3

3. 菓子箱

3. Boxes

4

JAPANESE SWEETS

ちとせ
CHITOSE

1

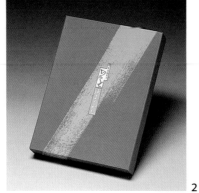

2

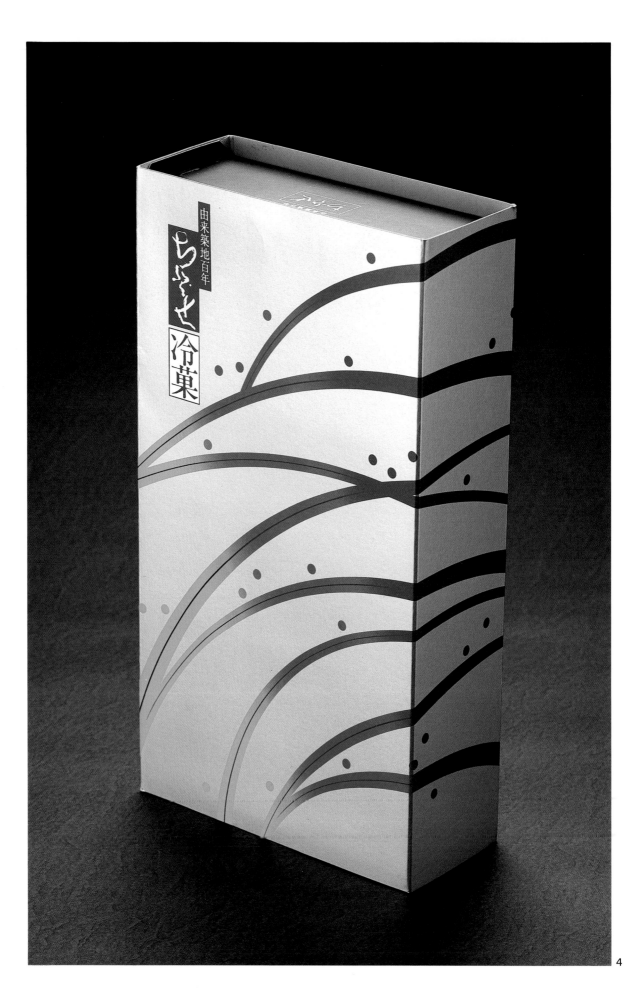

4. 菓子箱

4. Box

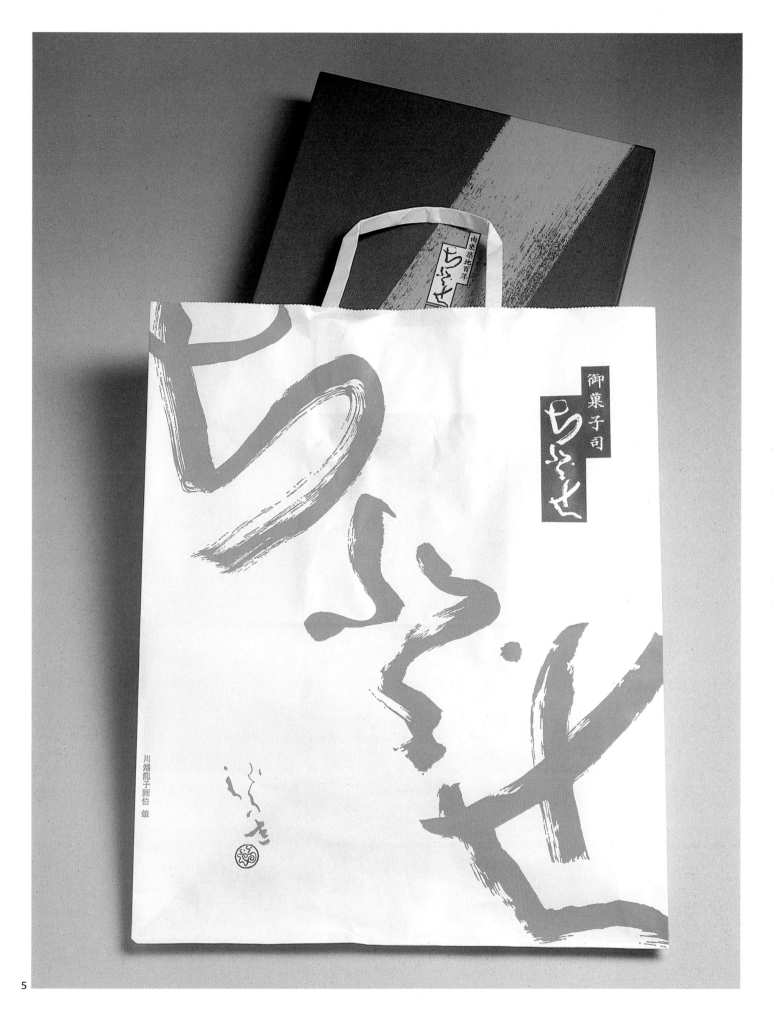

5. ショップバッグ、菓子箱

5. Shopping bag, box

JAPANESE SWEETS

叶 匠壽庵
KANOU SHOJUAN

PL （株）叶 匠壽庵
AD （株）叶 匠壽庵
D （株）叶 匠壽庵

PL Kanou Shojuan Co., Ltd.
AD Kanou Shojuan Co., Ltd.
D Kanou Shojuan Co., Ltd.

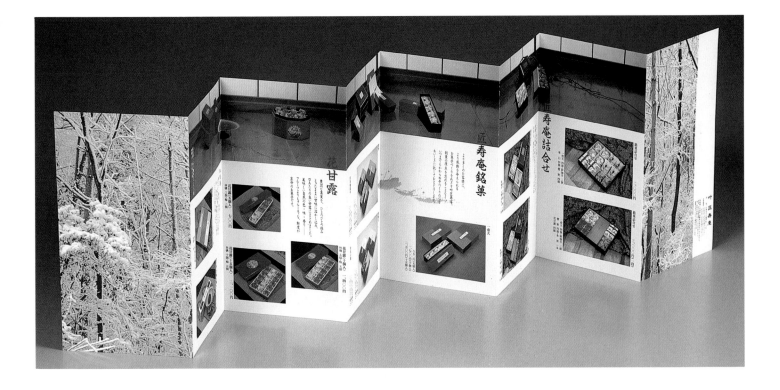

1

2

JAPANESE SWEETS

麻布和泉家
AZABU IZUMIYA

PL （株）和泉家　企画室
AD （有）アルマ・クリエーターズ、
　　山田良一
D 　（有）アルマ・クリエーターズ、
　　松本由佳里

PL Planning Sect., Izumiya Co., Ltd.
AD Ryoichi Yamada, ALMA Creators
　　Ltd.
D 　Yukari Matsumoto, ALMA Creators
　　Ltd.

1. パンフレット
2. パンフレット

1. Brochures
2. Brochures

1

2

3

3. ショップバッグ、懸紙
PL （株）和泉家　企画室
AD　篠田桃紅
書　篠田桃紅

3. Shopping bag, gift wrapping papers
PL　Planning Sect., Izumiya Co., Ltd.
AD　Toko Shinoda
Calligraphy Toko Shinoda

4

4. お月見用パッケージ箱（上）
PL （株）和泉家　企画室
AD （有）アルマ・クリエーターズ、松本由佳里
D 　プロジェクト T、田代玲子
七五三用パッケージ3種
PL （株）和泉家　企画室
AD （有）アルマ・クリエーターズ、松本由佳里
D （有）アルマ・クリエーターズ、松本由佳里

4. Package for the Moon Viewing Party (top)
PL Planning Sect., Izumiya Co., Ltd.
AD Yukari Matsumoto, ALMA Creators Ltd.
D Reiko Tashiro, Project T
　 3 Package for the Celeblation of a Child's
　 third,fifth and seventh years on November 15
PL Planning Sect., Izumiya Co., Ltd.
AD Yukari Matsumoto, ALMA Creators Ltd.
D Yukari Matsumoto, ALMA Creators Ltd.

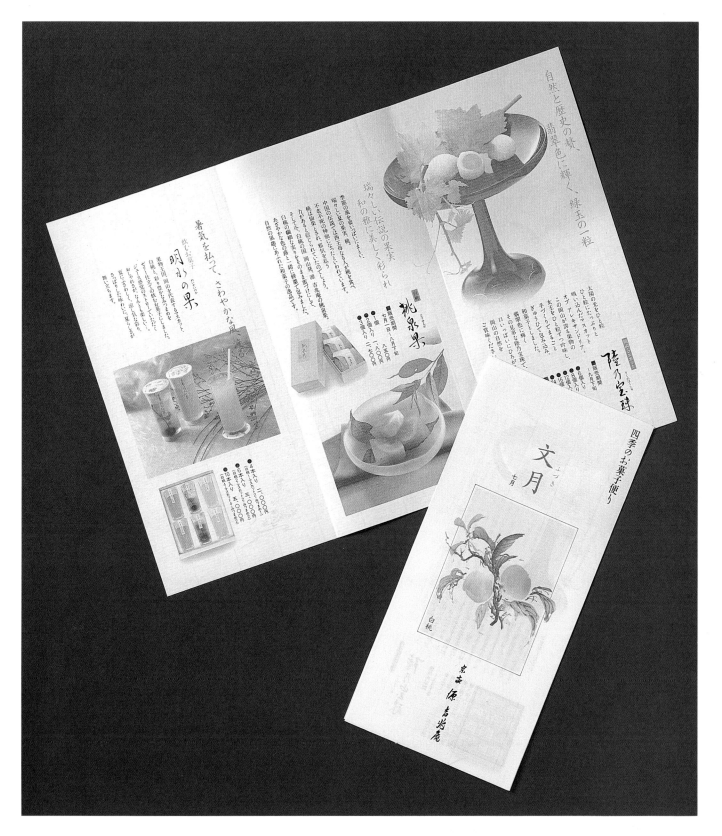

PL （株）源吉兆庵
AD （株）源吉兆庵
D I.D.A

PL Minamoto Kitchoan Co,. Ltd.
AD Minamoto Kitchoan Co,. Ltd.
D I.D.A

パンフレット
Brochures

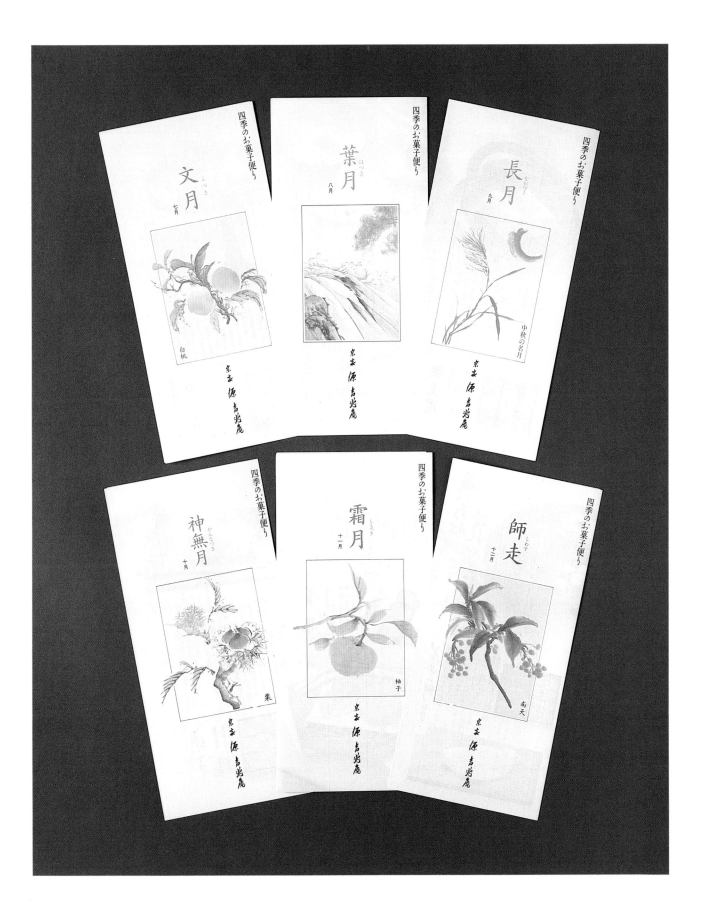

JAPANESE SWEETS

匠家花々亭
SHOKE KAKATEI

1.パンフレット
PL （株）パックペッカー
AD 山本良一
D 山本良一、水村満、後藤純也、
朝倉多民子

1.Brochures
PL Pack Pecker Co.,Ltd.
AD Ryoichi Yamamoto
D Ryoichi Yamamoto, Mitsuru
Mizumura, Junya Goto, Tamiko
Asakura

1

2

1, 2. 菓子箱（上）　　　　2. 菓子箱（下2つ）
PL （株）パックペッカー　　PL （株）パックペッカー
AD 山本良一　　　　　　　AD 山本良一
D　山本良一、水村満、石飛博光　D　山本良一

1, 2. Boxes (top)　　　　2. Boxes (others)
PL Pack Pecker Co., Ltd.　PL Pack Pecker Co., Ltd.
AD Ryoichi Yamamoto　　AD Ryoichi Yamamoto
D　Ryoichi Yamamoto, Mitsuru　D　Ryoichi Yamamoto
　Mizumura, Hakko Ishitobi

3. 菓子箱
PL （株）パックペッカー
AD 山本良一
D 山本良一、岸本太郎

3. Boxes
PL Pack Pecker Co.,Ltd.
AD Ryoichi Yamamoto
D Ryoichi Yamamoto, Taro Kishimoto

銀座鹿乃子
GINZA KANOKO

PL （有）鹿乃子
AD （有）鹿乃子
D （有）鹿乃子

PL Kanoko Ltd.
AD Kanoko Ltd.
D Kanoko Ltd.

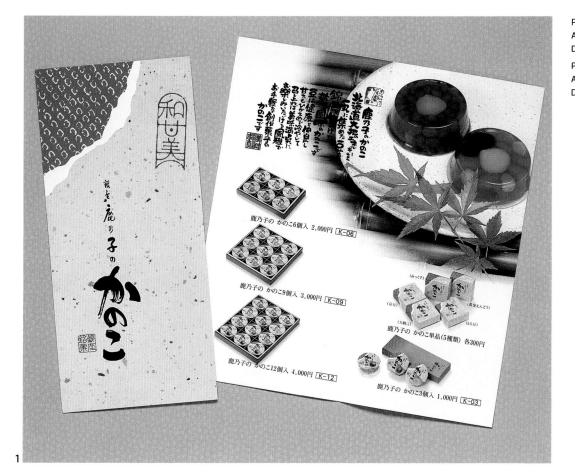

1. パンフレット
2. パッケージ

1. Brochures
2. Packages

虎屋
TORAYA

1. パンフレット
PL （株）虎屋、香村さやか
AD （株）アドマルク、高野倉善教
D （株）アドマルク、高野倉善教

1. Brochures
PL Sayaka Kamura, Toraya
Confectionery Co., Ltd.
AD Yoshinori Takanokura, ADMARK
Co., Ltd.
D Yoshinori Takanokura, ADMARK
Co., Ltd.

2. 懸紙
PL （株）虎屋 販売促進部
AD 永井鐵太郎
D 永井鐵太郎

2. Gift wrapping paper
PL Toraya Confectionery Co.,Ltd.
AD Tetsutaro Nagai
D Tetsutaro Nagai

2

2. 菓子箱
PL （株）虎屋　販売促進部
AD　永井鐵太郎
D　永井鐵太郎

2. Boxes
PL　Toraya Confectionery Co.,Ltd.
AD　Tetsutaro Nagai
D　Tetsutaro Nagai

PL　（株）高研、柳瀬　昇
AD　（株）高研、柳瀬　昇
D 　（株）高研、柳瀬　昇

PL　Noboru Yanase, Koken Co., Ltd.
AD　Noboru Yanase, Koken Co., Ltd.
D 　Noboru Yanase, Koken Co., Ltd.

パンフレット
Brochures

銀のぶどう
GIN-NO-BUDO

1. パンフレット
PL （株）グレープストーン・菓子企画部
AD （株）グレープストーン・菓子企画部
D （株）グレープストーン・菓子企画部

1. Brochures
PL Grape Stone Co., Ltd.
AD Grape Stone Co., Ltd.
D Grape Stone Co., Ltd.

JAPANESE CAKES

2〜10
PL （株）グレープストーン・菓子企画部
AD （株）ミックブレインセンター
D 　（株）ミックブレインセンター

PL Grape Stone Co., Ltd.
AD MIC Brain Center Co., Ltd.
D 　MIC Brain Center Co., Ltd.

2. パンフレット
2. Brochures

2

3

4

5

6. パンフレット
7. パンフレット

6. Brochure
7. Brochure

9. 菓子箱、パンフレット
10. 菓子箱

9. Box, Brochure
10. Boxes

JAPANESE CAKES

樹庵
JUAN

1. パンフレット
AD （有）プランテーション、奥山晶子
D 企画工房、上村昭二

1. Brochures
AD Akiko Okuyama, Plantation Ltd.
D Shoji Kamimura, Kikakukobo

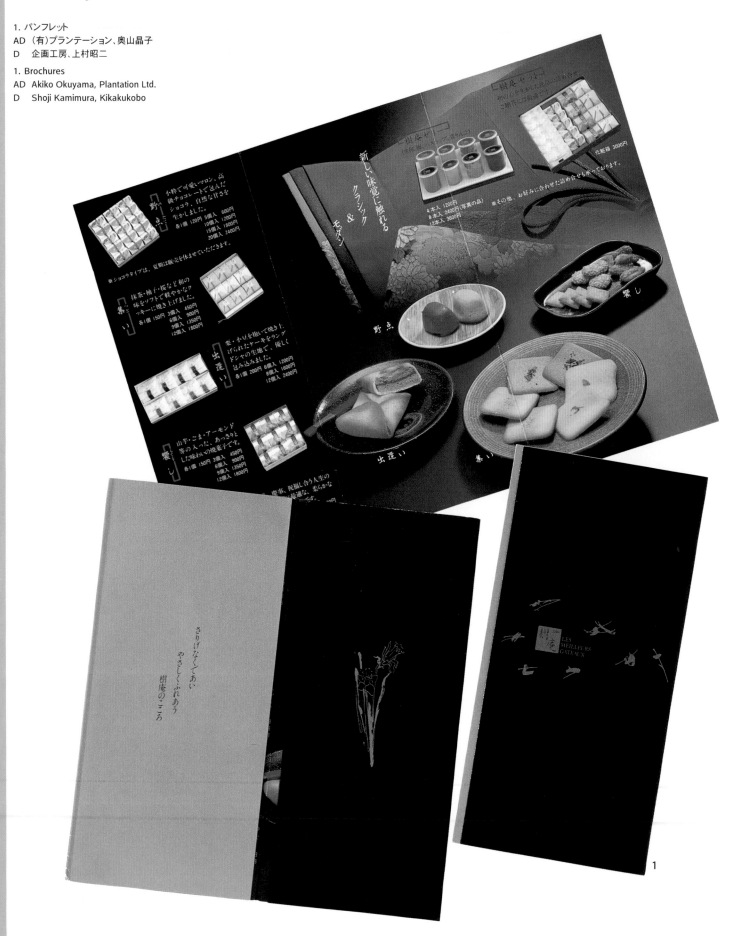

1

2. 菓子箱、パッケージ
D 企画工房、上村昭二

2. Box, packages
D Shoji Kamimura, Kikakukobo

199

赤坂柿山
AKASAKA KAKIYAMA

PL 佐竹起造、荻野寿子
AD 佐竹起造
D 佐竹起造

PL Kizo Satake, Hisako Ogino
AD Kizo Satake
D Kizo Satake

1. パンフレット

1. Brochures

2. 菓子箱

2. Boxes

RICE CRACKERS

銀座江戸一
GINZA EDOICHI

AD イプス・デザインズ、平野吉雄
D イプス・デザインズ、平野吉雄
AD Yoshio Hirano, IPCE Designs
D Yoshio Hirano, IPCE Designs

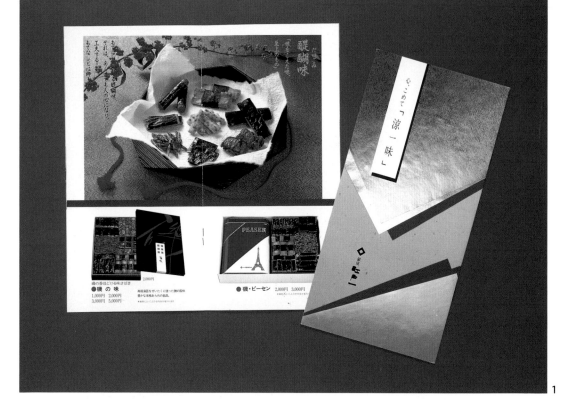

1. パンフレット
2. 缶、パッケージ

1. Brochures
2. Cans, packages

銀座花とみ
GINZA HANATOMI

AD 矢澤省三、(有)矢澤デザイン事務所
D 矢澤省三、(有)矢澤デザイン事務所

AD Shozo Yazawa, Yazawa design office Ltd.
D Shozo Yazawa, Yazawa design office Ltd.

1

2

1. パンフレット
2. 缶

1. Brochures
2. Cans

赤坂中央軒本店
AKASAKA CHUOKEN HONTEN

PL　（株）中央軒本店
AD　（株）サム・プランニング
D　　土江　理

PL　Chuoken Honten Co., Ltd.
AD　Sam Planning Co., Ltd.
D　　Osamu Tsuchie

1. パンフレット、菓子箱
1. Brochures, box

2

RICE CRACKERS

銀座　松崎煎餅
GINZA MATSUZAKI-SENBEI

PL　（株）松崎商店
AD　（株）松崎商店
D　（株）松崎商店

PL　Matsuzaki Shoten Co., Ltd.
AD　Matsuzaki Shoten Co., Ltd.
D　Matsuzaki Shoten Co., Ltd.

1. パンフレット

1. Brochures

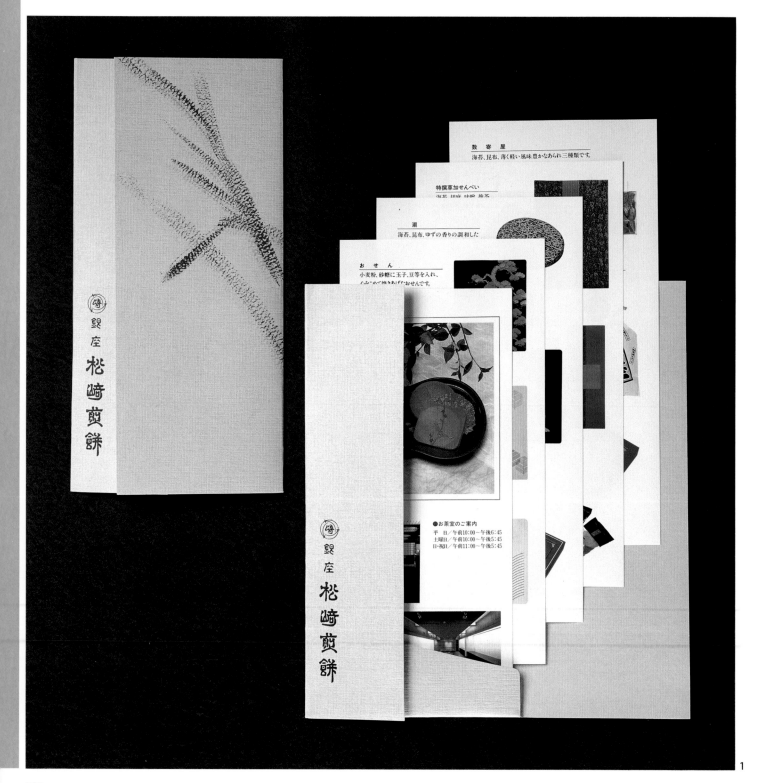

1

RICE CRACKERS

嵯峨野松風
SAGANO MATSUKAZE

PL （株）松風屋
AD （株）松風屋
D　（株）デザイン　アイ

PL　Matukazeya Co., Ltd.
AD　Matukazeya Co., Ltd.
D　 Design Ai Co., Ltd.

1. パンフレット

1. Brochures

MILLET-AND-RICE CAKES

常盤堂雷おこし本舗
TOKIWADO
KAMINARIOKOSHI
HONPO

PL （株）常盤堂雷おこし本舗
AD （株）常盤堂雷おこし本舗
D （株）常盤堂雷おこし本舗
PL Tokiwado Kaminariokoshi Honpo Co., Ltd.
AD Tokiwado Kaminariokoshi Honpo Co., Ltd.
D Tokiwado Kaminariokoshi Honpo Co., Ltd.

1. パンフレット

1. Brochure

2. パンフレット
D 石原喜雄（故人）

2. Brochure
D Yoshio Ishihara (deceased)

3. 菓子箱、シール

3. Box, take-out-bag for cakes, seals

4

CASTELLA

福砂屋
FUKUSAYA

PL 森田敏夫、（株）電通九州
AD 大坪数馬、アド・ノック
D 大坪数馬、アド・ノック

PL Tosio Morita,Dentsu Kyushu Co., Ltd.
AD Kazuma Otubo, AD･NOK
D Kazuma Otubo, AD･NOK

1. パンフレット

1. Brochures

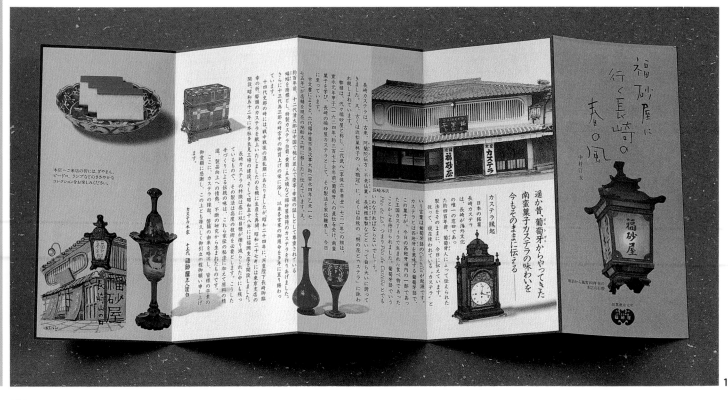

1

2

2, 3. 菓子箱、包装紙
PL （株）福砂屋
AD （株）福砂屋
D （株）福砂屋

2, 3. Boxes, wrapping paper
PL Fukusaya Co.,Ltd.
AD Fukusaya Co.,Ltd.
D Fukusaya Co.,Ltd.

INDEX & DIRECTORY

索引・住所

INDEX

赤坂柿山	〒107東京都港区赤坂3-6-10　電話(03)3585-9990
赤坂中央軒本店	〒176東京都練馬区豊玉北2-21-11　(株)中央軒本店　電話(03)3992-6111
麻布和泉家	〒106東京都港区西麻布1-7-5　(株)和泉家　電話(03)3404-8811
アンテノール	〒650兵庫県神戸市中央区中山手通1-22-13　電話(078)242-0656
アンの館	〒164東京都中野区本町4-32-3　電話(03)3384-7021
アンリ・シャルパンティエ	〒659兵庫県芦屋市公光町7-10-101　電話(0797)31-8315
池ノ上ピエール	〒155東京都世田谷区代沢3-42-8　電話(03)3421-6023
一番館	〒650兵庫県神戸市中央区元町通1-8-5　電話(078)391-3138
今田美奈子ティーサロン(原宿・薔薇の館)	〒150東京都渋谷区神宮前1-15-15　電話(03)3470-6528
ヴァローナ	〒107東京都港区赤坂8-7-18　ハイトリオ赤坂8丁目502号　電話(03)5474-7745
ヴィタメール	〒650兵庫県神戸市中央区中山手通1-22-13　電話(078)242-0656
エーデルワイス	〒650兵庫県神戸市中央区中山手通1-22-13　(株)スイス菓子エーデルワイス　電話(078)242-0656
叶　匠壽庵	〒520-22滋賀県大津市大石龍門町285　電話(0775)46-5300
カフェ ラ ミル	〒107 東京都港区南青山2-31-8　電話(03)3796-5260
鎌倉五郎本店	〒248神奈川県鎌倉市小町2-9-2　(株)鎌倉座　電話(0467)24-4433
銀座江戸一	〒104東京都中央区銀座8-5-12　(株)江戸一本舗　電話(03)3572-2246
銀座鹿乃子	〒104東京都中央区銀座5-7-19　電話(03)3572-0013
銀座花とみ	〒104東京都中央区銀座8-5-12　(株)江戸一本舗　電話(03)3572-2246
銀座松崎煎餅	〒104東京都中央区銀座4-3-11　(株)松崎商店　電話(03)3561-9811
銀のぶどう	〒166東京都杉並区阿佐ヶ谷南1-33-2(株)グレープストーン　電話(03)3316-0003
クレッセント	〒105東京都港区芝公園1-8-20　クレッセントハウス内　(株)クレッセント　電話(03)3436-3211
クローバー	〒106東京都港区六本木7-15-10　(株)ふらんす菓子　クローバー　電話(03)3404-9681
コート・ド・フランス	〒104東京都中央区銀座8-6-20幸佑ビル1F　サンアンドドニ(株)　電話(03)3573-3223
小岩井乳業	〒100東京都千代田区丸の内2-4-1　丸ビル3F　電話(03)3215-5271
ゴディバ	〒102東京都千代田区麹町5-7紀尾井町TBRビル601　電話(03)3234-1755
ゴンチャロフ	〒657兵庫県神戸市灘区船寺通4-2-8　電話(078)881-1188
嵯峨野松風	〒604京都府京都市中京区西ノ京小堀町2-10　電話(075)821-8412
サンジェルマン	〒213神奈川県川崎市高津区溝口1059　電話(044)833-2411
シェ松尾	〒104東京都中央区銀座6-8-7　交詢社501　(株)松尾企画　電話(03)5568-4736
資生堂パーラー	〒104東京都中央区銀座8-8-3　電話(03)3572-2121
シベール	〒104東京都中央区豊海町3-16(株)二幸　電話(03)3534-0482
樹庵	〒165東京都中野区松が丘2-4-14(株)ロイスダール　電話(03)5343-8131
匠家花々亭	〒222神奈川県横浜市港北区太尾町413-2　電話(045)546-3434
仙太郎	〒600京都府京都市下京区寺町通り仏光寺上ル　電話(075)344-0700
ダロワイヨ	〒104東京都中央区銀座2-6-16　電話(03)3564-2931

ちとせ	〒104東京都中央区築地1-9-4　電話(03)3541-0510
鶴屋吉信	〒602京都府京都市上京区今出川通堀川西入　電話(075)441-0105
ドゥバイヨル	〒105東京都港区虎ノ門2-3-13　片岡物産(株)　電話(03)3502-0261
常盤堂雷おこし本舗	〒111東京都台東区浅草3-6-1　電話(03)3836-5656
虎屋	〒107東京都港区赤坂4-9-22　電話(03)3408-4121
ノイハウス	〒150東京都渋谷区渋谷2-12-24　日本ノイハウス(株)　電話(03)3498-5348
パティスリーキハチ	〒107東京都港区南青山4-18-10(株)キハチアンドエス　電話(03)3403-4771
パティスリー・ラ・マーレ・ド・チャヤ(日影茶屋)	〒240-01神奈川県三浦郡葉山町堀内16(株)チャヤレストランシステムズ　電話(0468)75-8166
フーシェ	〒141東京都品川区西五反田2-29-5　日幸五反田ビル　電話(03)3969-8762
ブールミッシュ	〒213神奈川県川崎市高津区上作延539　電話(044)853-6253
福砂屋	〒850長崎県長崎市船大工町3-1　電話(0958)21-2938
不二家	〒104東京都中央区銀座7-2-17　電話(03)3572-4174
ぶどうの木	〒166東京都杉並区阿佐ヶ谷南1-33-2　(株)グレープストーン　電話(03)3316-0003
フランセ	〒221神奈川県横浜市神奈川区反町3-23-19　電話(045)342-5261
ブリアン　アヴニール	〒250神奈川県小田原市栄町2-6-12(株)三旺物産　電話(0465)24-4343
フレイバー	〒482愛知県岩倉市井上町字流87　(株)フレイバーユージ　電話(0587)38-0077
ペルティエ	〒150東京都渋谷区神宮前6-2-9　電話(03)3499-4791
ホテル　センチュリー　ハイアット	〒160東京都新宿区西新宿2-7-2　電話(03)3349-0111
ポニー	〒154東京都世田谷区三宿1-7-1　電話(03)3421-0691
本高砂屋	〒658兵庫県神戸市東灘区向洋町西5-1　電話(078)857-3333
ボンム アリス	〒105東京都港区芝大門2-4-1 izumiビル1F(有)宝盛堂　電話(03)3431-3284
マキシム・ド・パリ	〒104東京都中央区銀座5-3-1 ソニービル　電話(03)3562-6291
源吉兆庵	〒702岡山県岡山市築港新町1-24-21　電話(086)263-2651
無冬庵	〒658兵庫県神戸市東灘区向洋町西5-1　(株)本高砂屋　電話(078)857-3333
明治製菓	〒104東京都中央区京橋2-4-16　電話(03)3272-6511
メサージュ・ド・ローズ	〒150東京都渋谷区恵比寿南3-7-3 MUR代官山　電話(03)3711-6133
森永製菓	〒108東京都港区芝5-33-1　電話(03)3456-0112
モロゾフ	〒658兵庫県神戸市東灘区御影本町6 11 19　電話(078)822-5000
雪印乳業	〒160東京都新宿区本塩町13　電話(03)3226-2111
ヨックモック	〒107東京都港区南青山5-3-3　電話(03)5485-3333
ルノートル	〒170東京都豊島区東池袋3-1-1　サンシャイン60　38F(株)西洋フードシステムズ　電話(03)3984-0662
ロイスダール	〒165東京都中野区松が丘2-4-14　電話(03)5343-8131
六花亭	〒080-24北海道帯広市西24条北1-3-19　六花亭製菓(株)　電話(0155)37-6666
和光	〒104東京都中央区銀座4-5-11　電話(03)3562-2111

AKASAKA CHUOKEN HONTEN	Chuoken Honten Co., Ltd., 2-21-11, Toyotama-kita, Nerima-ku, Tokyo 176 TEL(03)3992-6111
AKASAKA KAKIYAMA	3-6-10, Akasaka, Minato-ku, Tokyo 107 TEL(03)3585-9990
ANTENOR	1-22-13, Nakayamate-dori, Chuo-ku, Kobe-shi, Hyogo 650 TEL(078)242-0656
AZABU IZUMIYA	Izumiya Co., Ltd., 1-7-5, Nishi-azabu, Minato-ku, Tokyo 106 TEL(03)3404-8811
BOUL'MICH	539, Kamisakanobe, Takatsu-ku, Kawasaki-shi, Kanagawa 213 TEL(044)853-6253
BOUTIQUE DE L'UM	4-32-3, Hon-cho, Nakano-ku, Tokyo 164 TEL(03)3384-7021
BRILLANT AVENIR	Sanoh Bussan Co., Ltd., 2-6-12, Sakae-cho, Odawara-shi, Kanagawa 250 TEL(0465)24-4343
BUDO-NO-KI	Grape Stone Co., Ltd., 1-33-2, Asagaya-minami, Suginami-ku, Tokyo 166 TEL(03)3316-0003
CAFÉ LA MILLE	2-31-8, Minami-aoyama, Minato-ku, Tokyo 107 TEL(03)3796-5260
CENTURY HYATT TOKYO	2-7-2, Nishi-shinjuku, Shinjuku-ku, Tokyo 160 TEL(03)3349-0111
CHEZ MATSUO	Matsuo Planning Co., Ltd., No.501 Kojunsha, 6-8-7, Ginza, Chuo-ku, Tokyo 104 TEL(03)5568-4736
CHITOSE	1-9-4, Tsukiji, Chuo-ku, Tokyo 104 TEL(03)3541-0510
CLOVER	Clover Co., Ltd., 7-15-10, Roppongi, Minato-ku, Tokyo 106 TEL(03)3404-9681
CÔTE DE FRANCE	Sun and Denis Co., Ltd., 1F, Koyu Bldg., 8-6-20, Ginza, Chuo-ku, Tokyo 104 TEL(03)3573-3223
CRESCENT	Crescent Co., Ltd., Crescent House, 1-8-20, Shiba-park, Minato-ku, Tokyo 105 TEL(03)3436-3211
DALLOYAU	2-6-16, Ginza, Chuo-ku, Tokyo 104 TEL(03)3564-2931
DEBAILLEUL	Kataoka & Co., Ltd., 2-3-13, Toranomon, Minato-ku, Tokyo 105 TEL(03)3502-0261
EDELWEISS	EDELWEISS Co., Ltd. 1-22-13, Nakayamate-dori, Chuo-ku, Kobe-shi, Hyogo 650 TEL(078)242-0656
FLAVOR	Flavor yuji Co., Ltd., 87, Aza-nagare, Inoue-cho, Iwakura-shi, Aichi 482 TEL(0587)38-0077
FOUCHER	Nikko-gotanda Bldg., 2-29-5, Nishi-gotanda, Shinagawa-ku, Tokyo 141 TEL(03)3969-8762
FRANÇAIS	3-23-19, Sori-machi, Kanagawa-ku, Yokohama-shi, Kanagawa 221 TEL(045)342-5261
FUJIYA	7-2-17, Ginza, Chuo-ku, Tokyo 104 TEL(03)3572-4174
FUKUSAYA	3-1, Funadaiku-machi, Nagasaki-shi, Nagasaki 850 TEL(0958)21-2938
GIN-NO-BUDO	Grape Stone Co., Ltd., 1-33-2, Asagaya-minami, Suginami-ku, Tokyo 166 TEL(03)3316-0003
GINZA EDOICHI	Edoichi Honpo Co., Ltd., 8-5-12, Ginza, Chuo-ku, Tokyo 104 TEL(03)3572-2246
GINZA HANATOMI	Edoichi Honpo Co., Ltd., 8-5-12, Ginza, Chuo-ku, Tokyo 104 TEL(03)3572-2246
GINZA KANOKO	5-7-19, Ginza, Chuo-ku, Tokyo 104 TEL(03)3572-0013
GINZA MATSUZAKI-SENBEI	Matsuzaki Shoten Co., Ltd., 4-3-11, Ginza, Chuo-ku, Tokyo 104 TEL(03)3561-9811
GODIVA	601, Kioi-cho TBR Bldg., 5-7, Koji-machi, Chiyoda-ku, Tokyo 102 TEL(03)3234-1755
GONCHAROFF	4-2-8, Funadera-dori, Nada-ku, Kobe-shi, Hyogo 657 TEL(078)881-1188
HENRI CHARPENTIER	7-10-101, Kinmitsu-cho, Ashiya-shi, Hyog 659 TEL(0797)31-8315
HON TAKASAGOYA	5-1, Koyo-cho-nishi, Higashinada-ku, Kobe-shi, Hyogo 658 TEL(078)857-3333
ICHIBAN KAN	1-8-5, Motomachi-dori, Chuo-ku, Kobe-shi, Hyogo 650 TEL(078)391-3138
IKENOUE PIERRE	2-42-8, Daizawa, Setagaya-ku, Tokyo 155 TEL(03)3421-6023
JUAN	Loisdar Co., Ltd., 2-4-14, Matsugaoka, Nakano-ku, Tokyo 165 TEL(03)5343-8131

KAMAKURA-GORO-HONTEN	Kamakura-Za Co., Ltd., 2-9-2, Komachi, Kamakura-shi, Kanagawa 248 TEL(0467)24-4433
KANOU SHOJUAN	285, Ryumon-cho, Oishi, Otsu-shi, Shiga 520-22 TEL(0775)46-5300
KOIWAI DAIRY PRODUCTS	3F, Marubiru, 2-4-1, Marunouchi, Chiyoda-ku, Tokyo 100 TEL(03)3215-5271
LE NÔTRE	Seiyo Food Systems Inc., 38F, Sunshine 60 Bldg., 3-1-1, Higashi-ikebukuro, Toshima-ku, Tokyo170TEL(03)3984-0662
LES PATISSERIES LA MARÉE DE CHAYA(HIKAGE-CHAYA)	Chaya Restaurant Systems Co., Ltd.,16, Horiuchi, Hayama-machi, Miura-gun, Kanagawa 240-01 TEL(0468)75-8166
LOISDAR	2-4-14, Matsugaoka, Nakano-ku, Tokyo 165 TEL(03)5343-8131
MAXIM'S DE PARIS	Sony Bldg, 5-3-1, Ginza, Chuo-ku, Tokyo 104 TEL(03)3562-6291
MEIJI SEIKA	Meiji Seika Kaisha Ltd., 2-4-16, Kyobashi, Chuo-ku, Tokyo 104 TEL(03)3272-6511
MESSAGE DE ROSE	MUR Daikanyama, 3-7-3, Ebisu-minami, Shibuya-ku, Tokyo 150 TEL(03)3711-6133
MINAKO IMADA TEA SALON (HARAJUKU-BARA NO YAKATA)	1-15-15, Jingumae, Shibuya-ku, Tokyo 150 TEL(03)3470-6528
MINAMOTO KITCHOAN	1-24-21, Chikko Shin-machi, Okayama-shi, Okayama 702 TEL(086)263-2651
MORINAGA & CO., LTD.	5-33-1, Shiba, Minato-ku, Tokyo 108 TEL(03)3456-0112
MOROZOFF	6-11-19, Mikage-honmachi, Higashinada-ku, Kobe-shi, Hyogo 658 TEL(078)822-5000
MUHOAN	Hon Takasagoya Co., Ltd., 5-1, Koyo-cho-nishi, Higashinada-ku, Kobe-shi, Hyogo 658 TEL(078)857-3333
NEUHAUS	Nihon Neuhaus Co., Ltd., 2-12-24, Shibuya, Shibuya-ku, Tokyo 150 TEL(03)3498-5348
PATISSRIE KIHACHI	Kihachi & S Co., Ltd., 4-18-10, Minami-aoyama, Minato-ku, Tokyo 107 TEL(03)3403-4771
PELTIER	6-2-9, Jingumae, Shibuya-ku, Tokyo 150 TEL(03)3499-4791
POMME ALICE	Hosei-do Ltd., 1F, izumi Bldg., 2-4-1, Shibadaimon, Minato-ku, Tokyo 105 TEL(03)3431-3284
PONY	1-7-1, Misyuku, Setagaya-ku, Tokyo 154 TEL(03)3421-0691
ROKKATEI	Rokkatei Confectionery Co., Ltd., 1-3-19, Nishi 24-jo kita, Obihiro-shi, Hokkaido 080-24 TEL(0155)37-6666
SAGANO MATSUKAZE	2-10, Kobori-cho, Nishinokyo, Nakagyo-ku, Kyoto-shi, Kyoto 604 TEL(075)821-8412
SAINT GERMAN	1059, Mizonokuchi, Takatsu-ku, Kawasaki-shi, Kanagawa 213 TEL(044)833-2411
SENTARO	Bukkoji-agaru, Teramachi-dori, Shimogyo-ku, Kyoto-shi, Kyoto 600 TEL(075)344-0700
SHISEIDO PARLOUR	8-8-3, Ginza, Chuo-ku, Tokyo 104 TEL(03)3572-2121
SHOKE KAKATEI	413-2, Futoo-cho, Kohoku-ku, Yokohama-shi, Kanagawa 222 TEL(045)546-3434
SIBELLE	NIKO Co., Ltd., 3-16, Toyomi-cho, Chuo-ku, Tokyo 104 TEL(03)3534-6482
SNOW BRAND MILK PRODUCTS	13, Honshio-cho, Shinjuku-ku, Tokyo 160 TEL(03)3226-2111
TOKIWADO KAMINARIOKOSHI HONPO	3-6-1, Asakusa, Taito-ku, Tokyo 111 TEL(03)3836-5656
TORAYA	4-9-22, Akasaka, Minato-ku, Tokyo 107 TEL(03)3408-4121
TSURUYA-YOSHINOBU	Imadegawa-Horikawa Nishi-iru, Kamigyo-ku, Kyoto-shi, Kyoto 602 TEL(075)441-0105
VALRHONA	VARI IONA JAPON S.A., Haitorio Suite 502, 8-7-18, Akasaka Minato-ku, Tokyo 107 TEL(03)5474-7745
	CHOCOLATERIE VARHONA , Zone Artisanale 26600 Tain L'hermitage France
WAKO	4-5-11, Ginza, Chuo-ku, Tokyo 104 TEL(03)3562-2111
WITTAMER	1-22-13, Nakayamate-dori, Chuo-ku, Kobe-shi, Hyogo 650 TEL(078)242-0656
YOKU MOKU	5-3-3, Minami-aoyama, Minato-ku, Tokyo 107 TEL(03)5485-3333

CAKES & SWEETS GRAPHICS
VISUAL PROMOTION FOR THE CONFECTIONERY INDUSTRY

Edited by **CAKES & SWEETS GRAPHICS Editorial Project + Media Factory Ltd.**

Art Direction & Design by **Flint Hill Ltd.**

Photographer: **Noritoshi Iwanaga**

Published by **MEISEI PUBLICATIONS**
3-11-1-203, Kandajinbo-cho Chiyoda-ku, Tokyo 101, Japan
Phone (03)5276-1941 Fax. (03)5276-1966

©1995 MEISEI PUBLICATIONS
Printed in Japan

ISBN4-938812-29-0 C3070 P16000E